Bulgarian WINE BOOK

Bulgarian

W  I

YASSEN BORISLAVOV

N E
BOOK

history

culture

cellars

wines

TRUD PUBLISHING HOUSE, 2004

Trud Publishing House is grateful
for the financial support of:

International Fair – Plovdiv

National Vine and Wine Chamber

BPS AG

Belvedere

Flyleaf: Traditional Bulgarian carpet (tcherga)

Page 2: Gold mask of Thracian king (fifth century BC) found in the Rose Valley, Bulgaria, in summer 2004

ISBN 954-528-478-1

contents

Chapter Three

Chapter Four

Heracles and Augae on silver plate from the Rogozen Treasure, fifth century BC

Wine as an Extension of the Personality and the Cultural Horizon of a Nation

Wine is as old as the world, yet it has never ceased to amaze. Today wine is just as fascinating as in the age of the righteous Noah, whom the Bible identifies as the first vine-grower, and just as capable of inspiring miracles such as the one at the wedding in Cana of Galilee. Wine continues to challenge science with its mysterious and noble nature.

No other beverage has had such great influence on the values and imagination of the European nations. Wine is not only part of everyday life and a source of livelihood. It is also present in mythology, religion, the arts, and literature. Invariably, it is a status symbol as well as an economic and legislative issue; in other words, it is part of politics. Wine often proves to be an asset to diplomacy. And last but not least, wine is an object of fashion.

In the history of civilisation there is a clearly defined geographical zone of wine and it is probably no coincidence that the countries from that zone have always been leaders in many other areas of life, too. Moreover, it is quite remarkable that the ages and countries that have respected wine have largely respected man, too. We need only remember the Classical and Hellenistic ages of Greco-Roman antiquity when culture and arts made to human measure flourished alongside remarkable winemaking skills. Or the age of the Renaissance, in which Bacchus came to life and dominated the works of Caravaggio, Michelangelo, Velásquez and many other artists with the same zestful resolve with which the heroes of Boccaccio, Rabelais, Chaucer and Shakespeare indulged their hedonistic passion for life that invariably included a passion for wine.

Wine is a universal metaphor in European culture and civilisation. In the course of its long and fascinating history, wine has acquired a well-defined 'human' profile to which this book would like to draw the reader's attention. Wine is not only a natural but also an intellectual product: to make an exceptional wine you need to imagine it first. Wine is an astute social psychologist as long as you know how to decipher its messages. The wines of the different nations usually carry some resemblance to their national character. That is why most French wines are aristocratic, German wines have a precisely modelled taste, Italian and Spanish wines are temperamental, whilst Californian and Australian wines are imbued with the challenge of state-of-the-art technologies.

For Bulgaria, wine has always been and will always be of special importance. Today, as in the past, it is not only and simply a source of livelihood, a solace in everyday life and a joy on festive occasions, but it is also part of Bulgaria's positive image as a civilised European country. Like the great European writers and artists of the Renaissance who contemplated the image of Bacchus, many leading figures in Bulgaria's nineteenth-century National Revival concerned themselves with some vinous issues too. The progress of the Bulgarian nation has always been reflected in the quality of its wine, and this is unlikely to change. Standards in the development of winemaking and viniculture have always been a measure of the well-being of society.

The main purpose of this book is to introduce traditional Bulgarian winemaking and its most recent trends even though we are clearly aware of the risks of such an undertaking: the processes under way in

Self-Portrait with Saskia, *Rembrandt*

the industry in the past few years have been particularly dynamic and this intense development is still continuing.

Knowing the wines of other countries and being able to judge fairly and honestly their advantages and disadvantages when compared to your own wine, means, in a sense, to be open to the world, to have a realistic perception of your own presence and worth among other nations. Producing wine that people in other countries recognise and enjoy means to be part of the world. Claiming that your wine is the best may be a quaint display of local patriotism, but it often betrays an inferiority complex and a lack of a proper sense of reality. Wine is an infinite domain of differences and that is precisely what makes its beauty even more expressive in an increasingly global world. Claiming that a particular wine is 'the best' betrays poverty of impressions and of the imagination. In other words, wine is a beautiful and elegant escape from provincialism.

A person's attitude to wine can provide an insight into that person's character. The ability to tell good wine from bad wine, to find the right words to describe and praise the former and to distance yourself from the latter means that you are a person with rich experience and culture. Wine is an extension of the personality, wrote Baudelaire. Let us add that the healthfulness of wine has invariably been one further reason for its popularity and value. Wine is a democratic alternative to spirits and drugs.

Yassen Borislavov

Dionysian scene on red-figured crater from an ancient necropolis near Burgas, Bulgaria, 420–410 BC

chapter 1

Wine and Civilisation

Wine is a cosmic problem

José Ortega y Gasset

A Gift of the Gods

The origin of wine is a mystery. It remains uncertain precisely where or when wine was first enjoyed. One thing, though, is certain – the first wine was not made, it simply 'happened' – and that is why it was perceived as a gift of the gods.

Although mythology implies that each ancient Eurasian people discovered wine independently, numerous linguistic, archaeological and historical studies have proved that winemaking spread largely as a result of cross-cultural influences.

The god Osiris taught the ancient Egyptians how to grow vines and make wine, but, according to some interpretations, this happened only after the sun god Amon-Ra, the creator of the world, introduced people to drinking and drunkenness. Some third-millennium BC murals in a tomb at Memphis depict scenes of grape harvesting and winemaking. A number of wine amphorae from the time of Tutankhamen (fourteenth century BC) have seals identifying the vintage, region and producer, allowing us to draw a rough map of wine appellations during the age of the Pharaohs. This map suggests that the best wines were produced in the Nile delta and the Memphis region.

According to the Bible, the first viniculturist was the righteous Noah, who, after the Deluge, 'began to be an husbandman, and he planted a vineyard; and he drank of the wine, and was drunken; and he was uncovered within his tent' (Genesis 9:20–21). Biblical archaeologists think that this vineyard was located within a fairly broad area around Mount Ararat and the southern Caucasus – that is, present-day Turkey, Syria and Armenia.

The ancient Greeks regarded wine as a gift of the god Dionysus. According to one popular myth, the first winemaker was King Oeneus or Oinos (his name is derived from the Greek word for 'wine'). His goatherd was Staphylos (the Greek for 'grapes'), who noticed that one of the goats would regularly wander off from the herd and come back later than the other goats in high spirits. The goatherd decided to follow the goat and saw it eating the fruit of a strange tree. Staphylos picked some fruit and took it to his master, who found that the squeezed juice of the fruit eventually acquired intoxicating properties. Oeneus offered it as sacrifice to Dionysus. The god rewarded the king by teaching him how to make wine and naming the drink after him, while the fruit was named after the goatherd Staphylos.

Roman mythology attributes the invention of wine to Saturn, the god of sowing and harvest, who, however, was later eclipsed by Bacchus (Dionysus).

***Bronze rhyton, Iran, fourth century** BC*

Some linguistic studies have attempted to link the origin of grapevines and wine to ancient India. They have established that the French word for grape, *raisin*, is derived from the Sanskrit *rasa* (grape) by way of the ancient Greek *ras* (grain) and the Latin *racemus* (a bunch of grapes). However, even though this etymology may seem logical in the case of *grapevine*, the search for a phonetic cognate of the Greek *oinos* and the Latin *vinum* in Sanskrit has not been so productive. These words lead, rather, to the Hebrew *yain* (wine), the Georgian *gvino*, and the Armenian *gini*. This shows that biblical archaeologists have apparently established the location of the first vineyard quite accurately.

Goblet of Pharaoh Thutmose III (1501–1447 BC)

The proposition that the roots of all civilisations genetically related to Europe are soaked in wine may sound like an overstatement, but it is correct. Wine was present even in the ancient cities of Mesopotamia, where, it has been proved, beer originated and played a predominant role. Herodotus, who visited those lands around 450 BC, claims that the local population were not familiar with the

Egyptian frescoes depicting grape-harvesting and wine-making scenes, twelfth century BC

Gold rhyton in the shape of a woman's head from the Panagyurishte Treasure, fourth century BC

grapevine and did not drink wine. However, it seems that, although he was not lying, the father of history was wrong. The people of Sumer and Akkad knew and valued wine highly, according to the French historian Jean Bottero ('La plus vieille histoire du vin', in *L'Histoire*, No. 228, 1999). Evidence of that has been found in cuneiform tablets dating from the third millennium BC. We have already mentioned that wine was produced in the region of Mount Ararat and the Caucasus, and it was transported in ten-litre clay jars by ship along the Tigris and the Euphrates. Some cuneiform records call it 'beer from the mountains'. Wine was traded actively, although it cost 250 times as much as wheat, and was only drunk on special occasions – weddings and other major feasts – and then only by royalty and the nobility. Kings gave their courtiers wine as a reward or a sign of esteem. Thus, the Sumerians and the Akkadians, who did not produce wine themselves, were the first to turn wine into a status symbol.

The Wine of the Ancient Greeks

In the ancient Greco-Roman world, wine was not simply a beverage. For the Greeks and the Romans it was the centre and driving force of civilisation, as well as its main symbol along with bread and olive oil. To a large extent, those three products determined the rhythm of ancient people's lives: they helped them become independent of nature, no longer simply collecting wild fruit but creating their own product or, in other words, culture. The production of wine, bread and olive oil strongly influenced the development of technologies and trade, while the feasts in celebration of their gods gave birth to the arts.

In a sense, the Homeric Greeks virtually originated from the vine and wine. The *Iliad* and the *Odyssey* describe the vine and wine tradition as already fully integrated into their everyday life and religious beliefs. In ancient geography the word *oinos* appears in the names of dozens of towns and

Homer

places. Vineyards are an organic part of the Aegean cultural landscape. Hesiod describes Crissa (the harbour of Delphi) as a 'town visible from a distance, steeped in vines'. In the *Iliad* wine is a ritual drink in both warring camps. Its quality is associated with the virtue of the heroes and it offers a foretaste of the expected victory. It is no accident that Homer includes a vine in the decoration of Achilles' shield. Even more interesting is his reference to vines trained on silver poles, making ancient viticultural techniques look quite modern.

Wine was a defining concept in the cultural world of the ancient Greeks; it was a measure of their superiority and it marked the boundary with the regions of hostile barbarians. Odysseus used Thracian wine to get Polyphemus the Cyclops drunk before blinding him.

The festivities in honour of Dionysus were celebrated across ancient Greece and participation in them was extensive, but, as many scholars observe, there was something quite distinctive about them – they were not 'merry' in the modern sense of the word but, rather, wild and dissolute.

Winemaking scene with sileni on Greek amphora, 530 BC

The son of Zeus and the mortal Semele was not like the other gods: he was more earthly and closer to people. He did not take part in the intrigues surrounding the Trojan War, and his place on Olympus seemed vacant. His cult was associated with the famous Eleusinian Mysteries and other secret religious rites of ancient Greece, which around the sixth century BC gave rise to the Dionysian festivals. The Great (City) Dionysia was celebrated at the end of March and in December, while the Little (Rustic) Dionysia was in late November.

Ritual performances and processions were more important in the worship of Dionysus than in any other cult. According to Aristotle's *Poetics*, the three main literary genres – poetry, tragedy and comedy – originated directly from them. More than any other god, Bacchus (as the Romans would call Dionysus) inspired in his worshippers a state of mystic ecstasy and unrestrained exaltation, in which wine undoubtedly played an important role. Wine helped ancient people transport themselves from their earthly, mundane existence to an ecstatic and epiphanic participation in the world of the

Satyrs crushing grapes, drawing on Greek vase, sixth century BC

gods. This was a time of primordial chaos in which there was no order, and therefore many things or almost anything was allowed. These festivals, involving phallic processions of masked satyrs and bacchantes, free-flowing wine and bawdy songs, gave birth not simply to bacchanalia (in the modern meaning of the word) but also to a lively, open and life-affirming culture that valued freedom above everything else. The writer Ortega y Gasset must have had this particular aspect of the Dionysia in mind when he wrote that for the ancient peoples 'wine was a wise, fertile and playful deity'. In the Classical and Hellenistic Ages, these festivals became increasingly secular in character. In addition to the obligatory dramatic performances, sophists and provincial philosophers demonstrated their rhetorical skills, their debates often degenerating into quarrels; poets recited verse; and there were also conjurors, soothsayers and, of course, merchants selling all sorts of merchandise. Fairs and carnivals, an important part of the calendar and culture of mediaeval Europe, originated from those festivals.

Another major contribution of the ancient Greeks to European civilisation was also directly associated with wine: the banquet or feast, which in the Classical Age (fifth–fourth century BC) became a central feature of ancient Greek democracy. This was not just a lavish banquet but also a ritual with its own rules, dramatic form and, occasionally, noble,

Bacchanalia

Dionysian scene on red-figured crater from an ancient necropolis near Burgas, Bulgaria, 420–410 BC

Scene from ancient Greek feast, drawing on plate, 470 BC

spiritual and public purpose – it was an experience of shared solidarity, community and joy.

The feast consisted of two parts: first, the participants would eat and then drink wine. The second part was called the *symposium* or *symposion*, when wine drinking was accompanied by music, poetry and dancing as well as discussion on all kinds of subjects, ranging from gossip to the abstract and the mystical – in other words, the ancient Greek banquet was not entirely unlike today's academic symposiums. The participants in every feast would elect a symposiarch – a master of ceremonies, who would set the pace of the pouring out of wine and the subjects of conversation, and would generally be responsible for the pleasant progress of the feast. As a rule, only men took part. Women (unmarried) appeared only as dancers, courtesans and flute-players. In fact, the symposium engendered one of the democratic values of the ancient world: the open discussion and solving of public problems. Through the symposium, wine gave birth to politics and advanced the development of poetry, as many poetic forms were created specifically to reflect the needs of the symposium. By creating a wisely peaceful and harmonious atmosphere around the table, the feast marked the boundary between the civilised and the barbarian worlds. To the ancient Greeks, 'Scythian drinking' meant not only 'drinking wine neat' – but also drunken behaviour that overstepped the limits of propriety.

This characteristically Greek interpretation of drinking ethics is illustrated by a poem by Anacreon (sixth century BC):

Boy! bring here a cup!
and
Boy! mix ten cups of water to five of wine
and
Boy! let me not shut my lips but let me drink
and drink and rage like
a frenzied Bacchus with
impunity.

Come, friends! let's not shout and scream
like Scythian drunks
but
let us study our wine, friends,
and
*accompany its drinking with beautiful songs.**

Such banquets were held in various places. A banquet in a private residence would be held in the *andron*, that is, the men's quarters. Quite often, however, banquets were also staged in public buildings, where the local nobles would drink wine from *phials* while reclining on special beds or sofas called *kline*. This was one of the purposes of the *tholos* (a circular, domed building) in Athens, which served as a dining hall for the Athenian Senate. Larger feasts were also staged in the open air.

Bacchus in Rome

Unlike the Hellenic world, which, as argued above, was inspired by wine, during the first few centuries after Rome was founded (753 BC) the presence of the vine in the city was not particularly conspicuous. When Aeneas settled in the province of Latium, the inhabitants were not yet fully part of the wine culture. Wine consumption remained limited for quite a long time. Pliny the Elder writes that Romulus offered milk as a libation, while the law of another mythical Roman king, Numa Pompilius (eighth century BC), banned the pouring of libations of wine over the pyres of the dead. According to Pliny, it was only around 600 BC that the Romans started cultivating vines, no doubt under the influence of the Greek colonies in the southern peninsula. From the eighth to the third century BC, men under the age of 30 were not allowed to drink wine. For women the prohibition was total. Early Roman

**Translated by George Theodoridis*

Mosaic from Villa Constanza, Rome, fourth century AD

records tell of one Egnatius Metellius killing his wife because she had drunk wine, and being subsequently absolved by Romulus. The inexorable enemy of Carthage and advocate of the revival of strict ancestral custom, Cato the Elder (234–149 BC) advised any husband who caught his wife drinking wine to kill her. However, by the end of the republican period, wine had become part of everyday life not only for men but also for Roman matrons.

According to the French historian Pierre Grimal, world history changed the day the Greeks introduced their conquerors to the science of gastronomy. The earliest demonstration of power and influence through food dates back to the late second century BC. In addition to gold, silver, marble statues and live Greek philosophers, the victorious Roman legions brought back to Italy Greek culinary habits, including the taste for wine. The modest way of life characteristic of the age of the Punic Wars eventually gave way to a rather more refined style and diet. A hot supper (*cena*) now became the main meal of the day, which noblemen washed down with wine while reclining in the *triclinium* (dining-room). Wine also became part of the staple diet of the plebeians, as the following inscription on a lamp from northern Italy proves: *'Bread, wine and vegetables: the poor man's food.'* Horace also refers in a poem to bread, wine and vegetables as vital to life.

Unlike the Greek symposium, where wine was not drunk with food, in Rome wine became an essential part of the meal. This gave rise to the typical Mediterranean culinary tradition based on bread and wine.

During the life of Augustus (63 BC–AD 14), the capital city received wine from the four corners of the empire and gradually started developing a specialist wine vocabulary. Once again, the first examples of this can be found in the poetry of Horace, who defines Falernian wine as 'dry, strong and fierce'. Roman men demonstrated their social standing through their preference for particular wines and their ability to procure them.

According to Virgil (70–19 BC), there were as many kinds of wine as the grains of sand in the Libyan desert. Virgil must have been right, considering that one century later (AD 92), according to Suetonius in his *Lives of the Twelve Caesars*, the emperor Domitian ordered the destruction of half of all vineyards in the provinces of Gaul and Spain. According to Suetonius's friend Martialis, it was more profitable in Ravenna to own a reservoir than vineyards, as the price of water was higher than that of wine. Most historians from the period agree that this restrictive law was not particularly effective, and in 276 the emperor Probus revoked it.

By that time, wines from Gaul had become quite popular in Rome. According to Roger Dion, the first and still highly respected wine historian in France, two important French grape varieties were cultivated during that particular period. Allobrogica, later renamed Pinot Noir, was grown in the Rhône valley, while in the region of Burdigala (modern Bordeaux), the Celtic tribe Bituriges Vivisci (kings of the world) cultivated Biturica, now better known as Cabernet.

Medicine also contributed to the adoption of wine into the everyday life of ancient people. Hippocrates (460–377 BC), supported later by several other Greek physicians, noted the salubrious effect of fermentation in wine. Cato recommended particular wines as a cure for dysentery and constipation. The wines from the Alban Hills were believed to have a soothing effect. Asclepiades of Bithynia, a Greek physician who settled in Rome in the late second century BC, developed the existing knowledge considerably by trying to establish at what point wine stopped having a therapeutic effect and became harmful to the patient's health, as well as which wines should be used to treat particular diseases. The idea of wine as a prophylactic is attributed to him, along with the subsequent development of appellations of origin in Rome. Asclepiades was a friend of both the general Licinius Crassus and an epicure who was quite well known in his day, Sergius Orata. The three men would spend long nights at richly laden tables, discussing the qualities and ranking of food and wine in the empire. Some consider them to be the founders of two genres typical of the culture of the age: *censura culinarum* and *censura vinarum*.

Techniques and Tastes in Antiquity

What did ancient wines taste like, how were they made and when were they drunk? Most ancient writers provide some answers, be it directly or in passing. After Homer and Hesiod, the works of Herodotus, Theophrastus, Plato, Aristophanes, Plutarch, Strabo, Tacitus and Seneca, as well as later writers such as Aulus Gallius and Athenaeus, give us some idea of winemaking in the ancient world. Wine was present in the poetry of Archilochus, Alcaeus, Anacreon, Horace, Virgil and Ovid, as well as in the prose of Apuleius, Lucianus and Petronius. Particularly valuable descriptions of vinicultural and winemaking techniques were provided by the four great Roman natural scientists: Varro, Cato the Elder, Columella, and Pliny the Elder.

Today, it is difficult to form with any certainty opinions and judgements about the grape varieties of the ancient world. There must have been hundreds of varieties as early as the days of Homer. When Odysseus finally returned to Ithaca and had to prove to his father Laertes that he was really his son, Odysseus reminded him how, when he was still a little child, Laertes had shown him and named 'the fifty rows of vines' that he would bequeath to the boy, 'whereof each one ripened at diverse times, with all manner of clusters on their boughs'.

***Roman amphorae, first century* AD**

According to Theophrastus (*Enquiry into Plants*), the grape varieties in Greece were as many as the different types of soil. He recommended growing white grape varieties on slightly porous black soil that was sufficiently moist. Still, the ancient Greeks were well aware that water was not always good for the growth of vines and, according to Theophrastus, that was why they would plant barley and legumes between the vines to soak up excessive moisture. Opinions on the question of soil suitability for vine-growing differed, but that of Columella (first century AD) was closest to modern views: Columella recommended planting vineyards on land that was 'halfway between good and bad land'.

The choice of vine-training style depended on the climate. In Greece, particularly in the areas exposed to the north wind, the vines were trained in rows not higher than the average adult (*vinea*), while in Italy and, more specifically, in Campania they were trained to creep up trees (*arbustum*). This could be one of the reasons for the better quality of Greek wines. Thus, Pliny recorded that a diplomat by the name of Cineas, an envoy of the Epirote king Pyrrhus (known for his Pyrrhic victory), tried some Italic wine and declared that the vine that had produced it deserved to be hanged on a very high gallows. This style of vine training made picking grapes a dangerous job, and hired pickers would often stipulate that the vineyard owner would have to pay for their funeral in the event of an accident.

After the grape harvest, the Greeks sometimes fumigated their vineyards by burning dry branches and leaves. This protected the vines from frost and it is still done in many parts of Europe. In addition to standard vineyard operations such as pruning, nipping, and replanting, the Greeks also knew some methods of treating sick, yellowing vines. They drove iron nails into the trunks of such vines, left the nails in place for some time, and then removed them and filled in the holes with earth. Although this practice was associated with the belief in the magic power of iron, from a modern perspective it looks quite rational. The vines were most likely affected by chlorosis, a disorder caused by iron deficiency in the soil; therefore, the magic cure must have been effective.

In Greece, the grape harvest was usually in September. In his *Works and Days*, Hesiod recommended that grapes be harvested when Orion and Sirius reached the centre of the sky. Plato wrote that in his ideal state this custom should become law. The grape harvest was (and, in fact, still is) conducted in two stages – early and late harvesting, depending on the variety and the degree of ripening. In the third century AD, Athenaeus stated in his work *The Gastronomers* that the famous Falernian wine from Campania was of two kinds, sweet and sour. The wine was sweet if the harvest coincided with the warm southern winds and then the grapes acquired a darker colour. In all other cases, the grapes remained lighter in colour and the wine was tart.

The bunches were picked by hand or cut with vine-hooks. They were collected in wicker baskets or large skeps, as described by Varro in the first century BC (*On Agriculture*). Most authors recommended that the harvest should always start at the sunny side of the vineyard.

It was apparently common practice to dry the grapes for some time before proceeding to make wine. In *Works and Days*, Hesiod recommends leaving the picked grapes in the sun for ten days and for a further five days in the shade before crushing them and putting them in jars. The period of time the grapes were left to dry varied from place to place. On the island of Cos, for example, the grapes were left in the sun for three days only. The same technique is mentioned by Homer when he describes what Odysseus saw in the garden of Alcinous, the mythical king of the Phaeacians, on the island of Scheria (Corfu):

'There, too, hath he [Alcinous] a fruitful vineyard planted, whereof the one part is being dried by the heat, a sunny plot on level ground, while other grapes men are gathering, and yet others they are treading in the wine-press' (*Odyssey*, Book VII, 123-125).*

Nowadays, a similar technique is applied in the production of some sweet wines, such as Tokay, Marsala or Sauternes – in other words, it is obvious to the wine expert why at the subsequent feast in Alcinous's house Odysseus was offered 'honey-sweet wine' and why sweetness is the dominant feature of most descriptions of the taste of wines in Homeric times.

The actual practices of winemaking did not change significantly from antiquity to the nineteenth century. The grapes were trodden in wooden or stone tubs (*linos*). The wine press was introduced late, under Roman influence. This technological advance was first applied in the production of olive oil and later adapted to winemaking.

There were two kinds of wine: free-run wine (lightly pressed out) and press wine (pressed out from fermented grapes), which was stronger and tarter. Quite often the marc was not thrown away but soaked in water and used to produce a second run of wine. Varro describes this wine as suitable for slaves and livestock. By contrast, Cato the Elder advises giving slaves wine made from dried grapes of the inferior varieties. For that purpose, before the grapes were fully ripe, the bunches would be nipped without fully detaching them from the stem and left on the vine for some time. Those wines must have also been quite sweet.

The Greeks, like the Romans, preferred more aromatic wines and often flavoured their wine with various herbs, honey and aromatic resins during or after fermentation. If the wine was to be stored for a longer period of time, they added pine resin just before the end of fermentation. This specific resinous flavour was valued highly and has been preserved in modern Greek retsina. Another favourite nuance in the bouquet was the aroma of smoke. Roman and Greek authors note that some wines were left for a while in a smoke-filled room (*fumarium*).

Satyr with wine crater, Crete, sixth century BC

* *Translated by S. H. Butcher and A. Lang*

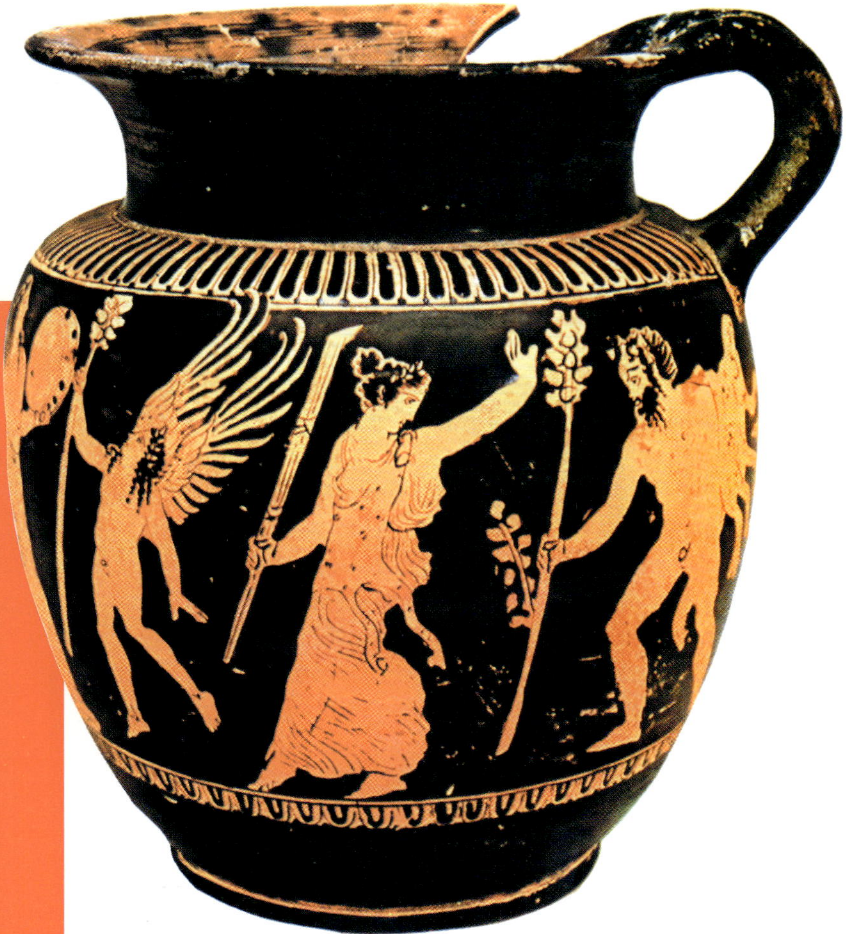

Scene depicting satyrs and maenads on red-figured oinochoe (wine jug) from an ancient necropolis near Burgas, Bulgaria

Ancient Greek amphora for wine transportation

Seawater was also added to some wines. Later authors such as Athenaeus attribute religious meaning to this practice and explain it by quoting an episode from the myth about Dionysus, who leapt into the sea to avoid being captured by Lycurgus. Apart from the mythological explanation, seawater must have given this wine something which it otherwise lacked. According to Pliny, seawater mellowed the taste of wine. The proportions varied from one region to another: on the island of Rhodes the amount of seawater added to wine was insignificant, but on Lesbos it reached up to 20 per cent, and on Cos even up to 50 per cent.

To restore spoiled wines, merchants would add wood ashes, powdered gypsum, alabaster or other substances rich in potassium carbonate, which neutralised the accumulated acetic acid. To mellow the acerbic and bitter taste, they also added grape juice concentrated by evaporation – a method still applied in modern wine production. Records also mention fining by adding white clay or egg white or by cooling, as well as filtration through linen cloth.

Most sources predating the first century BC leave no doubt about the superiority of Greek to Italic wines. At the feasts of Lucullus (106–56 BC), the most important toasts were raised with Greek wines. They were traded all over the Mediterranean world, and the prices of some vintages from Chios, Thasos and Cos were several times higher than those of local wines. The wines from Thasos were said to make the drinker rich, energetic and generous.

There are no records of counterfeits of Italic wines in Greece, but counterfeits of Greek wines in Italy were quite common. Some Roman writers offer recipes for preparing 'Greek wine' in places far away from Greece, giving us some idea about ancient winemaking practices. According to a recipe recorded by Cato the Elder, the wine should be boiled, diluted with brine, flavoured with herbs and left in a jar in the sun for two years. The result was wine from the island of Cos.

Later on, a certain balance between Greek and Italic wines was achieved. Around the first century BC, Roman winemakers started using Celtic oak casks, which improved the taste and reputation of Gallic wines over the next few centuries. The traditional sweetness was gradually replaced by a more complex taste (probably closer to that of modern dry wines), as clearly represented in Galen's classification (see p. 28).

In Greece, as in Rome, wine was produced and stored in large earthenware vessels called *dolia* with a capacity from 500 to 2,000 litres. Pliny recommends burying dolia holding weak wine in the ground, and keeping those holding strong wine in the open air. In Campania the noblest wines were kept outdoors, as it was believed that nothing could be better for them than the effect of the sun, moon, rain and winds.

Wine was transported in amphorae and served in craters (large, wide-mouthed bowls), invariably mixed with water. The practice of mixing wine with water was preserved throughout antiquity and over the following centuries. The proportion depended on the taste and the occasion. In *Works and Days* Hesiod advises mixing three parts of water with one part of wine. In the *Odyssey* Homer mentions 'honey-sweet' dark Thracian wine, one part of which was mixed with twenty parts of water.

In Horace's time, it was customary to mix twelve parts of wine with nine parts of water, nine being the number of the Muses. Some people, however, preferred their wine stronger and mixed twelve parts of wine with three parts of water, three being the number of the Graces.

We can only speculate about what the average consumption of wine was in antiquity. According to Cato, allocating the equivalent of 260 litres of wine a year per capita to slaves was not considered excessive. Free citizens were undoubtedly entitled to a much larger quantity. Novalis Torquatus (first century BC), proconsul of Gaul, is said to have been given the nickname Tricognius because of his habit of downing three *cognia* (ten litres) of wine at a gulp. In his youth the emperor Tiberius (reigned AD 14-37), who also bore the name 'Nero', was also strongly addicted to wine and was known as Biberius Mero (from *bibo*, to drink, and *merum*, pure wine). Seneca mentions two prefects of Rome from the same period, Lucius Piso and Tiberius Cos, who often got so drunk that they had to be carried out of the Senate. Still, this did not prevent them from being respected as good citizens and wise magistrates. People in antiquity showed remarkable tolerance towards this particular vice. They tried to apply an ideal of moderation and harmony both to the arts and to drinking. However, unlike the ideal proportions of the human body determined with mathematical precision by the Greek sculptor Polyclitus (fifth century BC) in his treatise *The Canon*, moderation in wine drinking has always been strictly individual. Those who criticised Polyclitus because his statues were admirable in form but lacking in expression and did not depict the true character of people would have hardly said the same of the transformations inspired by wine. Wine invariably succeeds in exposing and displaying a person's individual character traits, albeit not necessarily in an admirable form.

The fall of Rome in AD 476 halted the development of viticulture and wine production in Western Europe for a long time. But the idea of the universality of the Roman Empire was to be taken up and advanced by the Christian Church, which, like the ancient Greeks and Romans, had a special attitude to wine. The old maxim *Ubi ecclesia, ibi Roma* (Where the church is, there is Rome) proved fully valid for wine, too. Looking back at European history today, we may safely paraphrase this as *Ubi vinum, ibi Europa* (Where wine is, there is Europe).

Galen of Pergamum

Galen's Classification

The first classification of wines in antiquity, which, as it happens, is quite close to our modern understanding, was offered by Galen of Pergamum (second century AD), personal physician to the emperor Marcus Aurelius, and author of remarkable medical treatises, as well as a fervent wine lover, connoisseur and taster. According to Galen, wines vary firstly by *colour*, secondly by *taste*, thirdly by *thickness*, fourthly by *aroma*, and fifthly by *strength*. By colour, he classified wines as *white, black, golden, amber*, and *red*, noting that there are many intermediate shades. By taste, Galen classified wines into two groups, *sweet* and *tart*, again noting that there are intermediate variants. He added that there are also wines which combine the two tastes and that, finally, there is a taste called *spicy*. By thickness, he classified wines as watery and concentrated but, once again, pointed out that there are intermediate variants (*On Antidotes*).

The 100-Year-Old Opimian Falernian: Myth or Reality?

'Wine lives longer than poor little man', says one of Petronius's characters (*Satyricon*) when he sees 'some glass bottles carefully sealed with gypsum', with a label bearing the following inscription fastened to the neck of each one: 'Opimian Falernian: 100 years old.' 'Why is the wine that is drunk at your table older than you are yourself?' Seneca asked his friend Gallio (*On the Happy Life*). Indeed, some ancient vintages were remarkably long-lived, although most wines seldom lasted until the next grape harvest. According to Pliny, wines from Campania were at their best after the fifteenth year, while those from Pompey reached perfection in the tenth year, and further ageing added nothing to their quality. The reason for that lies in the vinification technique and type of wine in those days.

In 1991 Hervé Durand, an owner of vineyards near Nîmes (southern France), conducted an experiment in ancient winemaking by strictly following the prescriptions in Columella's treatise on agriculture from the first century AD. (The experiment is described by A. Tchernia, 'Comment on a retrouvé le gout du vin romain', in *L'Histoire*, No. 241, 2000.) The must was thickened to two-thirds of its original volume by slow boiling (*defrutum*), fined with salt and gypsum, and then flavoured with several quinces, iris roots and trefoil leaves, and left to mature in accordance with the ancient rules. The final product was reminiscent of sherry and some naturally sweet wines from the Rhône valley. Obviously, the desired taste of most ancient wines was the result of intense and continuous oxidation processes in direct contact with air – a practice still applied in the production of wines such as sherry (also known as sherris or Jerez), port or Madeira to achieve their distinctive *rancio* flavour. Over the years they developed a specific, slightly tart flavour, which inspired one Attalus, quoted by Seneca, to say 'Even the memory of lost friends is not as pleasant as the bitter flavour of old wine.'

Stored in large earthenware vessels (*dolia*), the wine developed a white film of skin produced by natural yeasts (the 'flower of wine') which imparted a distinctive flavour in the course of ageing. This is implied in a verse by Ovid, who mentioned 'carefully tended flowering wines with a white veil'. 'If the wine has white mould on the surface, that is well', Pliny explained. 'If the mould is red, this means that the wine cannot last long.'

This technique allowed some vintages to last for many years, improving as they matured. Aged in this way, they also increased their alcohol content as a result of evaporation. Strange as it might seem at first glance, the frequent references to wines that were ten years old or more in the writings of various authors are quite likely to have been true. The fabled 100-year-old Opimian Falernian (of vintage 121 BC, the year that Opimius was consul) served at Maecenas's table and extolled by so many of his contemporaries must have actually existed. In Pliny's time it was already 200 years old, and, according to him, it was so 'thick and sweet, like bitter honey', that it could neither be diluted with water nor drunk straight.

Wine Appellations in Horace's Poetry

The works of Quintus Horatius Flaccus (65–8 BC), better known as Horace – one of the greatest ancient poets of the age of Julius Caesar and Augustus, who, even though he was the son of a freed slave, was highly educated, exceptionally talented and recognised as an arbiter of taste, a friend of Virgil and Maecenas, and an ardent admirer of Bacchus – offer sufficient evidence to allow us to draw a comparatively accurate map of wine appellations in the early Roman Empire. Wine flows as freely in Horace's odes, satires and epistles as it must have flowed in real life. Horace mentions thirteen typical wines from Italy, Greece and Egypt in a context that gives a rough idea of their ranking by quality and price. In one of his works, the poet asks whether poems improve with time, like wine. His answer is that it depends both on the wine and on the poems; some survive the test of time while others do not. Considering that Horace's poems have survived the test, we can most probably trust his judgement on wines, too. His thirteen wines are as follows:

Horace

Sabine: a common country wine from the Sabini mountains. The lightest of all Italic wines, served for popular and everyday consumption.

Caecuban: produced in the region of Caecubus in southern Latium. One of the best Italic wines. In his odes Horace refers to 'the treasured Caecuban' and to the Caecuban it was a 'shame to broach' before the day of Caesar's victory.

Cossian White: produced on the island of Cos in the Aegean. One of the most distinguished wines in the ancient world.

Calenian: produced in Calenum (now Calvi) in Campania; a superb wine.

Falernian: the most famous of all Italic wines. Produced in the province of Falernum, northern Campania, from different grape varieties. The volcanic soil in the region is one of the reasons for its good quality.

Formian: from the town of Formia, near Naples. High-class wine.

Chian: from the island of Chios in the Aegean. Very high class. Describing Caesar's feast to celebrate the conquest of Spain, Varro writes that the feasters drank amphorae of Falernian but jugs of Chian.

Massic: good-quality wine from the Massic Hills in Campania. 'Howe'er men call your Massic juice, / Its broaching claims a festal day', Horace writes in one of his odes.*

Alban: from the Alban Hills southeast of Rome. Comparatively good.

Lesbian: from the island of Lesbos. Fine and highly prized.

Veian: lower-quality wine produced in the town of Vei in Etruria.

Mareotic: produced in the province of Maraea, near Alexandria. The best of all Egyptian wines.

Surentan: produced in the town of Surentum (now Sorento) in Campania. Judging from the context, it must have been good.

Naturally, these were only some of the wines typical of the age that left a lasting impression on the palate. No doubt there would have been many local wines that were not part of the imperial wine trade because of their inferior or mediocre qualities. Horace also mentions mixing Falernian and Chian, as well as mixing Falernian with honey, a popular practice in his time. A century later, Pliny classified Italic wines into four categories depending on their quality, and added another dozen or so appellations. According to Pliny, the wines of the ancient world that were noteworthy were 80 in all, two-thirds of which originated in Italy.

**Translated by John Conington*

The Mystic Wine of the First Christians

The role of wine in the everyday and spiritual life of mediaeval people was as important and ever present as in antiquity. In the Christian cosmos, wine is one of the symbols of the faith. The Christian attitude to wine, however, was entirely different from the pre-Christian. This is not the wine of pagan festivities nor the ecstatic wine of Greek Dionysia and Roman Saturnalia, but a new wine of sobriety, catharsis and anxious expectation of the Day of Judgement.

The Bible abounds in parables and allegories related to the life of vines and fermented grape juice – there are more than 400 references to them in various contexts from the very first book, Genesis, to the very last one, The Revelation of St. John the Divine (Apocalypse). For Christians, wine is a universal metaphor of life. In the Old Testament, wine is a symbol of the relationship between man and God and of divine grace; in the Gospels it symbolises the blood of the Saviour shed for the remission of sins, while in the Revelation it is a sign of divine wrath.

God did not grant the first people either vines or wine. It was only after the Deluge that Noah

Christ in Wine Press, ***Germany, c. 1500***

'began to be an husbandman, and he planted a vineyard; and he drank of the wine, and was drunken; and he was uncovered within his tent' (Genesis: 20–21). His youngest son Ham, the father of Canaan, laughed at the nakedness of his father, but Noah's two older sons, Shem and Japheth, hastened to cover his nakedness. When Noah awoke from his drunken sleep, he learned what his youngest son had done and cursed Canaan to be 'a servant of servants' to his brethren. Thus, the first wine acquired part of the symbolic meaning of the forbidden fruit in the Garden of Eden. More significantly, God punished not the father's drunkenness but the son's ridicule, the disrespect for authority. Wine was a gift of God and a sign that from then onwards people were no longer doomed to a bleak life of endless work for their daily bread, but would also have holidays when wine would help them forget their cares and misfortunes. The essence of wine as represented in the Old Testament is expressed by King David: 'wine that maketh glad the heart of man' (Psalms 104:15). Wine is an integral part of the notion of well-being and is therefore frequently invoked in blessings, as Isaac blessed his son Jacob (Genesis 27:28): 'God give thee of the dew of heaven, and the fatness of the earth, and plenty of corn and wine.' Wine is part of sacrificial offerings and is sometimes called 'blood of grapes'. The Old Testament does not encourage drunkenness but counsels reasonable moderation.

Christ's first miracle was turning water into wine at the wedding in Cana of Galilee. It is not difficult to imagine the dramatic intensity and implications of the words of the Virgin Mary, who discreetly told Jesus and His disciples when they asked for wine at the wedding: 'They have no wine' (John 2:3). Here wine is the key not only to the happy conclusion of the wedding but also to everything that would be described by the Gospel writers.

At the Last Supper, Christ took the cup and gave it to His disciples, saying, 'Drink ye all of it; for this is my blood of the new testament, which is shed for many for the remission of sins' (Matthew: 26:28). In other words, for mediaeval Christians, wine was a symbol of atonement for the original sin and of salvation. It is part of the central sacrament in the liturgy, the Holy Communion (the Eucharist), in which wine and bread symbolise the dual, divine and human, nature of Christ; wine is the symbol of His divine nature, and bread of His human nature.

In the Revelation, vine and wine metaphors are used to depict first a depraved and dissolute way of life, and then the righteous wrath of God: 'Babylon is fallen, is fallen, that great city, because she made all nations drink of the wine of wrath of her fornication', says one of the angels. The Day of Judgement is compared to the grape harvest. 'Thrust in thy sharp sickle, and gather the clusters of the vine of the earth; for her grapes are fully ripe', another angel says. 'And the angel thrust in his sickle into the earth, and gathered the vine of the earth, and cast it into the great winepress of the wrath of God. And the winepress was trodden without the city, and blood came out of the winepress, even unto the horse bridles, by the space of a thousand and six hundred furlongs' (Revelation 14:8, 18–20).

The attitude of mediaeval Christians to wine was deeply ambivalent. They could not deny themselves wine for the reasons listed above. To abhor the substance of the Eucharist would be heretical, but to enjoy it, to take pleasure in its taste and gladly drown care in wine, was a grave sin, too. Mediaeval Christian ethics was based on the renunciation and avoidance of all pleasures of the flesh. The Christian was torn between wine and abstention – that is, between need and sin – and this state was described very accurately by St. Augustine, the leading authority on questions of faith in Western Europe in the early Middle Ages. As he wrote in his *Confessions*: 'And health being the cause of eating and drinking, there joineth itself as an attendant a dangerous pleasure, which mostly endeavours to go before it. ... Placed then amid these temptations, I strive daily against concupiscence in eating and drinking. For it is not of such nature that I can settle on cutting it off once for all, and never touching it afterward, as I could of concubinage. The bridle of the throat then is to be held attempered between slackness and stiffness.' It seems, though, that there were different opinions on the question of how tightly the bridle of the throat ought to be held in different countries and among different clerics.

In the chapter on 'How to Drink' in the *Rule of St. Benedict* (early sixth century), the founder of Western monasticism wrote that a quarter of a litre of wine a day is sufficient, but went on to make an important point: should the need arise, the abbot may increase the ration as long as there is no 'excess and drunkenness'. It seems that many bishops and abbots often used their discretion to determine exactly how much wine the monks should drink and precisely what 'excess and drunkenness' meant. According to the French historian Jean-François Gautier (*Histoire du vin*, Paris, 1992), that was the reason for the rise of the image of monks as tipplers, prevalent in French culture. It could be added that the phenomenon was certainly not limited to France. It must have been the commonly slack 'bridle of the throat' that prompted Pope Innocent III (1198–1216) to condemn priests who

Painting from Italian wall calendar, c. 1500

'belch' when blessing their flock because of the wine drunk the day before (*On the Miserable Condition of Man*).

It is certain that under the influence of the Church, between the fifth and the ninth centuries, the cultivated grapevine (*Vitis vinifera*) conquered vast new territories in Europe, far beyond the boundaries of the original Roman Empire. Wine slowly advanced in lands that previously had been traditional domains of ale and beer.

The culture of eating in Europe in the early Middle Ages was characterised by the triumph of wine as a beverage drunk not only on special occasions but on an everyday basis, according to the Italian historian Massimo Montanari ('Production, Structures and Food Systems in the Early Middle Ages', in *Food. A Culinary History*, 1999). Without belittling the presence of ale and beer, which have always been national drinks in the German and Anglo-Saxon part of Europe and, moreover, were also used in pagan rites, we must admit that wine ultimately won the war. It was recognised as the universal European drink not only because of its taste but, even more so, because of its canonisation by the Church. Depending on quality, wine could be both an everyday and a luxury beverage. In northern Europe, wine was by definition a drink for the elite. Peasants normally drank beer, a tradition which eventually spread south to the Mediterranean.

Monastic brotherhoods would play a remarkable part in the promotion of wine in Europe. Monastic cellars set the first wine standards and produced the first typical local wines, whose taste would later dictate wine fashions. The early rise of winemaking in France and other parts of the continent is associated with the large monastic orders of the Benedictines and the Cistercians. Benedictine brothers founded some of the best-known estates in Bordeaux, Burgundy, Champagne, the Loire valley and Provence. They are also famed for the liqueur Bénédictine, thus named by King Francis I in 1534 when he visited the abbey at Fécamp and was offered this remarkable drink. The missionary role of the Cistercians was just as remarkable. The very fact that the Cistercians founded Clos de Vougeot in 1336 is enough to prove that today's best and most expensive wines have their roots in a tradition established by the Church. 'For quality wines, abbeys in the Middle Ages would be what cooperatives would later be for ordinary wines', writes Jean-François Gautier.

The Wine of Lords, Serfs and Artisans

Engravings from the book **Opus ruralium commodorum,** *libri XII, 1498, University Library of Lausanne, Switzerland*

Two other important factors charted the course of European winemaking from the twelfth to the eighteenth century: the feudal aristocracy and the nascent capitalist market. In the twelfth and thirteenth centuries, monastic cellars supplied the lords – kings, princes or counts – who would eventually oust the Church from its position of power but would not stop loving wine and seeing its qualities and prestige as a symbol of their own prestige.

As in antiquity, social hierarchy inevitably produced a wine hierarchy. In the age of the Crusades, wine was an element of knightly honour on a par with horses, castles and weapons. The phrase 'bread, meat and wine' is commonly used in literature to describe all that a knight errant needed to live in dignity.

The history of burgundy is quite typical of the evolving attitude to wine in the courts of the European nobility. Burgundy largely owes its viticultural fame to the counts of the House of Valois, who, between the twelfth and the fifteenth centuries, invested much effort in improving the quality of local crops and probably with some justification claimed the title of 'masters of the best wines in the Christian world'. In 1395 Philip the Brave issued a decree ordering the uprooting of 'the insidious variety called gaamez [Gamay], which yields very bad wines in abundance'. This marked the beginning of the cultivation and selection of the still dominant variety, Pinot Noir. The region also owes its success to the numerous wine fairs (the first one opened in Mâcon in 1340), as well as to the commercial flair of the Burgundians, who started producing wines for specific markets comparatively early in history.

In 1351 French merchants were prohibited from selling wine from one vine region under the name

of another, and in 1360 the Royal Council of France classified wines on the market in three categories, setting a price range for each category.

A thirteenth-century French poem entitled 'The Battle of Wines' (*Le Bataille des vins*), describing a contest between wines of different origins and vintages at the court of King Philip Augustus, mentions as particularly distinguished among the whites the wines from Moselle and Alsace, La Rochelle, Chablis and Bonnes. The poet also defends enthusiastically the wines from the region of Paris (Île-de-France), which were quite popular during the following centuries and 'clear as a tear'. At that time they were the only wines designated as *vins de France*. These were the famous clairettes – light and fresh, on the border between rosé and red. (They are not to be confused with 'claret', as the British call some wines from Bordeaux, even though their names have a common etymology.) In 1642, when the Seine and Loire rivers were connected by a navigable canal, and wines from the Beaujolais region started flowing towards Paris, their fame gradually declined. Incidentally, almost all major vine regions in Europe are located in the valleys of navigable rivers, such as those of the Dordogne and Garonne in Bordeaux, and the Rhône in Burgundy and Provence, as well as the Loire, Rhine, Moselle, and Danube. The rivers were an important factor in the gradual growth of the wine trade, which, however, still remained relatively limited in mediaeval times. In the Middle Ages, most small and medium-size producers made wine mainly for their personal needs, selling wine only if they had a surplus.

Some of the impetus for the growth of winemaking was the result of the Great Plague of 1348, which reduced Western Europe's population by about a third. Only a year later, wages in farming and craftsmen's workshops had doubled and by the end of the century quadrupled. This process naturally led to an improvement in the quality of life, which, invariably, was reflected in the stan-

Engravings from the book **Opus ruralium commodorum**, *libri XII, 1498, University Library of Lausanne, Switzerland*

dards of consumption. Thus, wine gradually became more accessible and, perhaps, resulted in expectations of wine quality becoming somewhat higher, too.

It would be difficult to judge with any degree of precision the quality of wines up to the end of the sixteenth century. Naturally, some would have been better than others. The better ones were served at the tables of the gentry, while the rest, usually diluted with water, brightened up the daily life of the commoners. It would probably be somewhat overoptimistic to claim that any wines of particular vintages and origins were of exceptional quality. Neither the technology required for their production nor the social processes necessitating their appearance were in place. It would be naïve to expect high quality in wine in an age which did not yet know the fork (forks were not introduced in France until the seventeenth century), and most recommendations in court manuals on good manners advised, 'Do not spit on the table! Do not put chewed food back in the bowl! Wipe your mouth before drinking from a shared cup!'

Most wines did not last long and were finished by the following summer. Vintages that were three or four years old or more tended to be an exception. That is why around the year 1500 a cask of good young Bordeaux cost fifty livres, while a cask

Grape Harvest, *engraving by Johann Sadeler, late sixteenth century*

Illustrations to French manual on barrel-making, 1540

The King Drinks,
Italian miniature, sixteenth century

of old Bordeaux cost six livres. Even as late as the seventeenth and eighteenth centuries, some people still firmly believed that four- or five-year-old wines were rubbish. The attitude to older wines started changing gradually at the end of the seventeenth century when the practice of fumigating casks with sulphur was introduced in winemaking. This new practice was called 'Dutch matches', and winemakers probably owed it to Dutch merchants.

Vinification techniques did not change significantly from late antiquity to the mid-nineteenth century. Grapes were trodden or pressed with wooden presses (disputes of what was better continued right until the mid-nineteenth century), then fermented in wooden vats, and stored and traded in casks. Winemakers applied also well-known techniques from the past, such as racking, fining and filtration, by more or less primitive means.

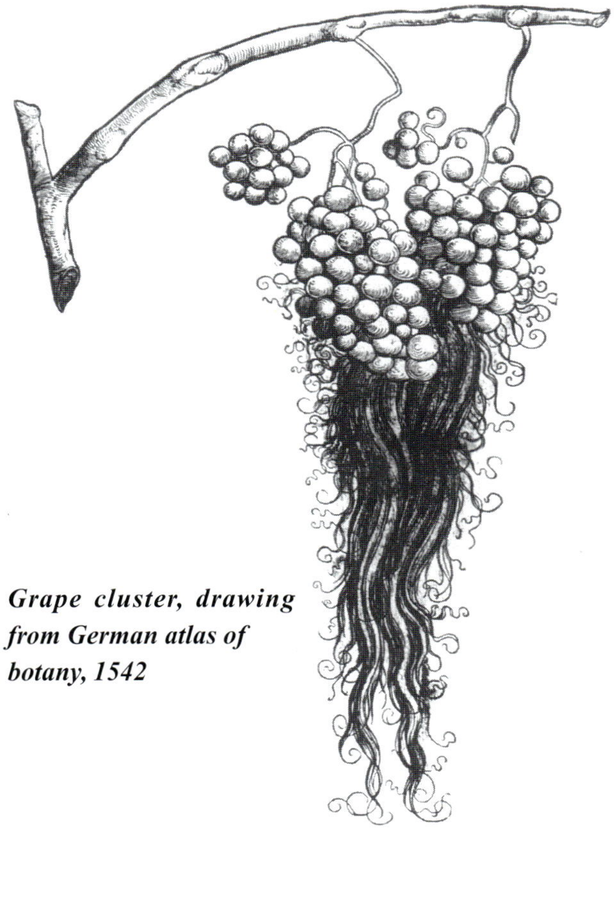

Grape cluster, drawing from German atlas of botany, 1542

Grape Harvest, ***Lukas von Valckenberg, 1585***

The quality of wine obviously depended above all on the grape variety, climate and soil.

In the Middle Ages, wine continued to be considered a healthful product. Some new ideas were added to the list of cures inherited from the late antiquity, in which wine was a main ingredient. It was popularly believed that 'through its warm nature, wine strengthens the body, helps digestion and banishes care'. A treatise on eating of 1542 states that moderate drinking raises the spirits and improves cardiac action. 'The finer the wine, the better the disposition of the spirit', claimed its author. According to Montaigne, the Parisian doctor Jacques Dubois (1478–1555) advised 'startling' the stomach with wine at least once a month, in order to prevent its laziness.

As in antiquity, wine continued to be flavoured with honey, herbs and resins, and was invariably diluted with water. Antoine Furetière notes in his *Dictionnaire universel* (1690) that 'only drunkards fail to dilute their wine'. That was done not only for considerations of taste but also of hygiene. The antiseptic properties of wine had already been discovered. Perhaps adding water also made the high acidity of some wines more palatable.

How much wine did mediaeval Europeans drink? The quantity varied in different countries and periods. In the twelfth and thirteenth centuries, the average consumption per capita in some regions of Italy approximated 260 litres a year. In the mid-seventeenth century, the annual consumption in Valladolid (Spain) was 100 litres, while on the eve of the French Revolution Parisians drank around 120 litres a year. In the north, consumption was considerably lower. The absence of wine was compensated for by beer, mead and cider. In all regions of Europe, wine consumption fluctuated from one period to another. Throughout the Middle Ages and right until the end of the nineteenth century, wine remained both luxury and nourishment in a considerable part of Europe. It often provided the missing calories; according to Fernand Braudel, that was why its price fell whenever the price of wheat rose.

Why Do Roman Catholics Celebrate Communion with White Wine and Orthodox Christians with Red Wine?

The colour of wine used in the celebration of Holy Communion is not specified in the Gospels. Considering that wine is a symbol of the blood of Christ, it should presumably be red. Up until the eleventh century, canon law decreed that only wine from grapes could be used in the holy liturgy, without specifying any further details. The Catholic Church, however, introduced changes to both liturgy and dogma. One of those changes was the use of white wine in the celebration of Holy Communion. It is not known for sure exactly where and when white wine was used for the first time. Documents from the Council of Cologne (1280) note in passing that the Eucharist wine must differ from water, a detail which implies that white wine must have already been used in some places. A French manual on liturgy from the late thirteenth century recommends using the 'finest wine' and notes a significant disadvantage of red wine: it stains the vessels on the altar. In 1565 the Council of Milan addressed the question of the cleanliness of the antimension, the cloth upon which the chalice is placed. That was when white wine, which must have already been used quite widely in the celebration of the Eucharist, was first permitted officially. Still, the question of the colour of the wine remained a subject of controversy in the Catholic Church over the following century. It was settled finally in 1659 by the Council of Majorca, which decreed that all priests must use only white wine in the celebration of the holy liturgy. Western canonists are, generally, not concerned with the question of colour while Orthodox clerics believe that only red wine is suitable for the occasion.

Gold chalice, Byzantium, tenth century

Britain's Special Role

Britain, which has never been a major wine producer, has nevertheless played a significant role in the development of European winemaking. In this respect, too, Britain followed the philosophy that has invariably guided its foreign policy: through encouraging competition for the British market among individual producers and regions, it helped set and improve standards. Some of today's famous wine regions owe their success largely to the British public and its sometimes rather peculiar tastes. This applies particularly to the wines of Bordeaux and several other French regions (Burgundy, Champagne, Provence and the Loire valley), as well as to some Moselle, Alsace, Italian and Spanish wines.

After King Henry II married Eleanor of Aquitaine (formerly queen consort of King Louis VII of France) in 1152, the English court received as a dowry the Duchy of Aquitaine (now Bordeaux) and other domains in France. Even more importantly, after the royal marriage, French wines became fashionable across the Channel. Up until 1453, when France recovered Bordeaux after the end of the Hundred Years' War, the region was a main

Engraving from mediaeval French calendar, Paris, 1491

The Marriage at Cana *(fragment), Paolo Veronese*

supplier of wine for the English market. Bordeaux wine, however, remained in demand, regardless of the recurrent Anglo-French conflicts – taste can sometimes be even more conservative than British policy. A special fleet was set up to service the wine trade, and in 1373 it numbered 300 ships. Quite often the grape harvests were insufficient to meet demand on the English market and merchants offered wine of lower quality from peripheral regions (*haut pays*). The English called those wines 'claret'.

According to some sources from the period, the perfect wine worthy of the English palate had to be 'clear as the tears of a penitent to the very bottom of the glass, and green as buffalo's horn. On drinking it was to descend as impetuously as thunder, sweet-tasted as an almond, creeping like a squirrel, leaping like a roe-buck, strong as a Cistercian monastery building, scintillating like a spark of fire, subtle as the logic of the school of Petit-Pont in Paris, delicate as fine silk, and colder than crystal' (C. Anne Wilson, *Food and Drink in Britain*, 1976). This inspired description clearly suggests that the English liked wines that were tart and tannic or, in other words, young.

In the Elizabethan Age (1558–1603), most wines were imported from France, but there were also some from the region of the Moselle and Rhine, Crete, Spain, southern Italy and other countries.

The picture changed in the seventeenth century. Rising taxes on both sides of the Channel and the subsequent war of England and the United Provinces of the Netherlands against France (1689–1697) brought to London the fashion of sweet Portuguese wines from the Douro region fortified with brandy. Drinking port was regarded as virtually a patriotic duty.

In the drunken British eighteenth century, it was considered entirely normal for a gentleman to

An Election Entertainment, ***William Hogarth (1754)***

imbibe two or even three bottles of port with or after his dinner. Spanish Jerez (sherris or sherry), which was known as 'sack' as early as the reign of Henry VIII (1509–1547), became increasingly popular, too. Other wines gained from the complicated Anglo-French relations, among them Madeira, Malaga and the Italian Marsala. Meanwhile, many Britons – in particular, representatives of the upper classes – remained fervent lovers of some French wines and were willing to pay their high prices. This distinguished clientele enhanced the prestige of some of today's leading producers and appellations from Bordeaux, such as Chateau Haut-Brion, Chateau Margaux, Chateau Lafite and Chateau Latour, as well as some Burgundian brands.

The Wine of the Enlightenment

The birth of Europe's greatest wines (*grands crus*) coincided with the age of the Enlightenment and reflected its historical logic. The improved quality of wine ran in parallel with the demand for quality in all other spheres of life. The French ethnologist and sociologist Marcel Mauss argues that, 'The rise of civilisations is not driven by industry – its main engine is luxury.' According to the philosopher Gaston Bachelard, 'man is a product of pleasure, not of need'.

Peasant Family, ***Louis Le Nain***

Grape Harvest near Sorento, ***Italy, Jacob Philipp Hackert, 1784***

Western Europe's typical local *grands crus* date back to the late seventeenth and eighteenth centuries. An Italian dictionary of commerce from 1762 lists the majority of today's better known appellations, rating most highly the wines from Champagne and Burgundy, followed by Chablis, Pommard, Chambertin, Clos de Vougeot, La Romanée and others.

Royal courts and the rich bourgeoisie played a crucial role in this process by setting fashionable trends that were dutifully followed by the aristocracy. For example, in the age of the House of Valois, the most fashionable wines in France were those from Burgundy. Following the ascent of the Bourbons, interest gradually shifted towards the Loire valley. Under Louis XIII, red Burgundies came back into fashion. Later on, under Louis XIV, wines from Champagne entered the leadership contest but, according to Gilbert Garrier (G. Garrier, 'Naissance des grands crus', in *L'Histoire*, No. 213, 1997), a medical and trade lobby centred around the king's personal physician Guy Fagon succeeded in tipping the scales back in favour of Burgundy. To keep pace with changing fashion, winemakers had to improve techniques and, consequently,

Merry Company, *Jan Steen*

taste. The wines from Champagne, mentioned earlier, were not yet the later famous sparkling wines but ordinary still wines. The Benedictine monk Dom Pierre Pérignon, whom legend credits with the invention of champagne even though similar bubbly wines are known to have existed in Britain much earlier, actually devoted all his winemaking efforts to the production of a wine capable of competing with Bordeaux and Burgundy for the royal table.

Between 1668 and 1715, Dom Pierre Pérignon was treasurer of the Hautvillers Abbey near the town of Epernay in Champagne, and his duties included those of cellar master. This was how he discovered that, in springtime, some bottled young wines developed high carbon dioxide levels and changed in taste. Nowadays, it is quite easy to explain what caused this process. The cool climate in that northern region did not allow grapes to ripen quickly, so the harvest was comparatively late in the year. The winter frosts set in before the wine had fermented fully. The arrival of spring triggered secondary fermentation and the carbon dioxide trapped inside the bottles saturated the wine with lively bubbles. Dom Pierre Pérignon desperately tried to get rid of them. This 'flaw' gradually came to be regarded as an advantage, but it was not until a century later that champagne turned into a standard of good taste and social prestige. Like the mediaeval alchemists before him, in his quest for the perfect white wine, Pérignon chanced upon some practices that would leave a lasting imprint on winemaking over the next centuries. He was the first to start blending wines from different varieties, regions and vintages in an effort to improve quality. His other monumental contribution was the introduction of the cork stopper. Up until then, cork stoppers had been virtually unknown in France, even though they had been used in antiquity, as evident from the wine-merchant's house excavated in Pompey, as well as from an ode by Horace that describes Greek amphorae plugged with resinated corks.

During the 1730s the fame of champagne gradually grew, after Louis XV allowed the transportation of and trading in bottled wine, but it became truly fashionable across Europe only on the eve of the French Revolution. Even before it had conquered France completely, this rare and expensive wine caused a furore at the royal courts of Britain, Prussia, Austria and Russia, whilst the third president of the USA, Thomas Jefferson, introduced it to America. In the nineteenth century it was desired and valued across the world as a symbol of festive chic and aristocratic prestige, and the champagne label became more popular than Bordeaux and Bourgogne. Thus, the dream of the Benedictine monk came true, even though not at the Sun King's table.

In 1815 Talleyrand opened the Congress of Vienna with champagne. The role of champagne as a specifically European cultural icon is particularly notable in Russia. In the early nineteenth century, the Russian gentry perceived champagne as a symbol of modernity and European identity. It is, therefore, hardly surprising that in *Eugene Onegin* Pushkin mentions some brands that are still popular today, such as Veuve Clicquot and Moët.

Europe's greatest wines include Tokay, which was also known as *elixir imperial*. It was an important attribute of Habsburg diplomacy. Referring to Tokay and the empress Maria Theresa, Pope Benedict XIV exclaimed, 'Blessed be the earth that has produced it, blessed be the lady that sent it to me and blessed be I for having been able to try it.' Tokay had other fervent lovers among European royalty, such as Peter I, Catherine II, and Edward VII. Its virtues were also extolled by philosophers and writers like Voltaire, Dumas père, Anatole France, Goethe and Heine, while Rossini is said to have always had a glass of Tokay on his piano when composing.

Credit Is Dead Here, ***popular French engraving, seventeenth century***

The Topers, ***Diego Velásquez***

Vendor of glasses and bottles, French drawing, sixteenth century

Cellar Master, ***lithograph by Gustave de Galard***

Wine in the Industrial World

The beginning of the modern history of wine dates from the mid-nineteenth century. Several milestones mark a process that changed first the notions and then the very nature of wine.

The famous wine classification of Médoc (Bordeaux) was produced in 1855, whereby wines were classified into five categories by their origin, quality and price. In 1861 a similar classification was produced in Burgundy and, over the following years, in all other wine regions in France. This practice was eventually adopted by almost all wine-producing countries in Europe and was adjusted to reflect the specific local conditions. It marked the beginning of an ambitious and determined effort to introduce order and standards in the wine market over the following decades. This was an essential requirement of the capitalist market, as quality wines were no longer targeted at personages such as Pope John XXII, Louis XVI or Napoleon but at everyone who could afford them. In the industrial world wine had become a commodity no different from any other.

The nineteenth century saw the emergence of modern wine law, which was also governed by the needs of the capitalist market. Paradoxically, even though Europe had produced and drunk wine for almost three millennia, it was not until 1889 that a French law, known as the Griffe Law, codified the answer to the fundamental question, 'what is wine?' It first formulated the definition that is still used by all wine laws: 'Wine is the product obtained from the fermentation of juice from fresh grapes.' By the end of the twentieth century, winemaking across the world was to be subjected to hundreds of legal, technological, economic and health restrictions, rules and regulations, effectively leading to a situation where, as a French oenologist pointed out recently, to produce a new wine today one must meet more conditions than to open a nuclear power plant.

In 1863 intensive vine and wine exchange between the Old and the New World brought the insect pest phylloxera to Europe. The arrival of phylloxera would force producers to rationalise and restructure their operations by the end of the century. In many regions this meant not only replanting vineyards and grafting vines on to American rootstock, but also changing the variety structure and, consequently, changing wine.

Yet, the true revolution that made modern wine qualitatively different from anything before it came as a result of Louis Pasteur's research. In 1863 Pasteur published his *Studies on Wine, Its Diseases, and the Causes Which Provoke Them*. In this treatise he explained alcoholic fermentation as a biochemical process involving natural yeast. Even though some of his theses would later be contested and partially revised, this classic work did for wine production what Kant's *Critique of Pure Reason* did for European philosophy. Each of those two great minds gave the world the solution to a mystery that had fascinated humanity for centuries: Kant unravelled the cosmos and established that the place of God seemed to be vacant, and Pasteur revealed the nature of wine. After Pasteur, the quality of wine was no longer a matter of trial and error – it became the subject of a new science: oenology. In the late nineteenth and early twentieth centuries, many of Pasteur's disciples – Müller Thurgau and Osterwalder in Switzerland, or Gayon, Dubourg and Duclos of the Bordeaux school – would constantly shorten the distance between scientific laboratories and wineries. Their discoveries would introduce universally applied practices,

Wine Tasting, *José Benlliure y Gil*

The Red Vineyard,
Vincent van Gogh

Louis Pasteur

Wine cellar at Vinivel Ltd – Ivailovgrad, Southern Bulgaria

such as the use of thoroughbred strains of yeasts and control of fermentation by cooling, as well as sulphuring, aeration, and filtration.

Microbiology also helped reshape modern wine production by boosting technological development. The tortuous ancient methods of grape crushing and wine racking, applied up until the nineteenth century, were gradually replaced by automatic destemmers and crushers, pumps, rotary fermenters, vinimatics, filters and all the other equipment that can be seen in a modern winery.

Thus, in the nineteenth century, wine started to lose its mythical aura – no longer a gift of the Greek or Roman gods, the mystic Christian wine or the product of the enlightened taste of European royalty, wine gradually became an industrial and technological product. Its taste was no longer a miracle of nature because it could now be shaped and adjusted as required. Still, wine remained burdened with the cultural and mythological legacy of its long history. It is not accidental that when relations between the USA and France soured on the eve of the war in Iraq in the spring of 2003, journalists engaged in a cross-Atlantic verbal sparring match the main subject of which was wine rather than oil.

The modern progress of wine has greatly extended its geographical boundaries. Incidentally, wine has followed in the footsteps of the Europeans ever since the sixteenth century, when the first vineyards were planted in Argentina, Mexico and Chile and, a century later, in California and South Africa. It has invariably been regarded as a European presence outside Europe. Today, New World vineyards span vast territories on both sides of the equator, in America, Africa, Australia, New Zealand and other countries. Their wine is drunk around the world and, according to some international studies, has a market with an annual turnover of around 100 billion US dollars. It is an important part of the global economy, and this may well bring about its future metamorphosis.

At the dawn of the modern age, the 1855 classification of Bordeaux wines established the concept of the direct relationship between origin and quality, a concept which, until recently, survived uncontested. Today, some new winemaking theories are trying to prove that, like beer and Coca-Cola, wine cannot be restricted to a particular geographical region; that technology or, in other words, human intervention, is a more critical factor than nature. Whether this will be proved right or wrong is yet to be seen. The story is to be continued. The long-running saga of wine may take yet another twist with the arrival of a new player on the scene: Australian wine technology versus *La terroir français*. Still, even this could hardly be the final twist in the tale of a drink that is the source of so much wisdom, inspiration, energy and health, because wine, as José Ortega y Gasset puts it, is a cosmic problem.

chapter 2

Vinaria

Renaissance Wine: Ethics and Aethetics

Bacchus, ***Caravaggio***

The day may still come when science and, specifically, medicine will find a rational explanation for a phenomenon which the inquisitive contemporary observer can merely describe – namely, that periods in history when people drank more wine and had a more liberal attitude to this gift of nature were undeniably the most creative and productive both scientifically and artistically. The spiritual pulse of European culture seems to have always been attuned to and reflected in wine.

Such a statement seems easier to defend when applied to the Renaissance, when the spirit of Bacchus inspired joyfulness and revelry among the characters portrayed by both literature and the visual arts. It is quite easy to see how wine gradually gave rise to a new, unmistakably Renaissance, interpretation of ethics and aesthetics.

Nearly 150 years after Jacob Burckhardt's seminal study, *The Civilisation of the Renaissance in Italy* (1860), European scholarly tradition is still dominated by the concept of 'individualism' as the most characteristic feature of the age, offering the key to its interpretation and understanding. During the Renaissance period, a person ceased to exist solely as a member of a particular class, party or guild – that is, as a component of a collective entity – and became an individual with his or her individual feelings, passions and free will. One of the manifestations of this 'individualism', and a direct function of free will, was the Renaissance attitude to wine.

In the visual arts, the Renaissance figure of the drinker emanates vitality, nobility and inner harmony. This attitude is unmistakably present in the paintings of Rembrandt (*Self-Portrait with Saskia*), Caravaggio (various representations of Bacchus), Velázquez (*Los Borrachos*), and Jacob Jordaens (*The King Drinks* cycle, albeit with some reservations as to nobility), to name but a few.

Giovanni Boccaccio

Satyr, ***bronze, Andrea Briosco, sixteenth century***

Giovanni Boccaccio and the Modern Perception of Wine

In *The Decameron* by Giovanni Boccaccio – 'the last mediaeval and the first modern humanist', as many of his biographers choose to define him – wine is not only a common detail, but also a key to some of the main ideas conveyed by the book. Quite often, before going to bed, the characters spend some time over a bottle of good wine. Wine is an intrinsic element of their perception of beauty and harmony in life.

The Decameron (Eighth Day, Third Tale) describes a fictional country, Bengodi, where the vines are tied up with sausages, and a goose is sold for a penny with a gosling thrown in for free, there is a high mountain made of grated Parmesan cheese, and the people who live there do nothing but cook macaroni and ravioli, boiling them

The Young Bacchus, *Caravaggio*

with broth of capons. Not far from this mountain runs a fair river, the whole stream being pure white Vernaccia (a grape variety): 'None such was ever sold for any money, and without one drop of water in it.'*

One of the characters boasts in company that 'he had made such good wine, as God himself did never drink better'. As a result, he is summoned by the Inquisitor, whom he eventually manages to outwit.

Boccaccio created also one of the most memorable figures in Renaissance literature, the lover hidden in a wine butt (Seventh Day, Second Tale). Literary historians rarely miss the opportunity to point out that this motif is borrowed from the Roman author Apuleius (*The Golden Ass*), but it nevertheless remains inherently representative of the spirit of the new age. Incidentally, in addition to this borrowed motif, *The Decameron* offers evidence of further, more significant and meaningful continuity with antiquity. And this can hardly be surprising. Peter Burke writes in *The Renaissance:* 'What is most typical of the Renaissance movement is the enthusiastic attempt to revive another culture, to emulate antiquity in many different spheres and circles.' This effort led to a rebirth of architecture, the Latin language and the visual arts; it was all essentially the product of a new attitude to the individual and the world around him, which – as we shall see below – applied to wine, too.

It is not difficult to identify traces of the ethics and aesthetics of the ancient Greek symposium in the structure of *The Decameron*. The ten young people fleeing from plague-stricken Florence retire to the countryside and decide that in the course of ten days each of them must tell stories in turn, and they agree that throughout this time their company shall 'live in order and pleasure, acceptable to all, and without shame to any'. 'Order' and 'pleasure' were the two key words which also defined the Greek symposium as a forum for discussion with strictly established ethical standards and aesthetic aspirations. Boccaccio's characters decide that they will take turns as the elected king or queen for the day, an arrangement reminiscent of the equality of the participants in a feast in antiquity, as well as of the ritual hierarchy established through the election of a symposiarch (see also p. 20–21). The undertaking of the characters in *The Decameron* had clear aesthetic motives, too: they were fleeing from Florence, where 100,000 people had died from the plague in

* *All quotes from* The Decameron *translated by John Florio*

just a few months, the streets were strewn with corpses, and a horrible stench and groaning arose from the dead and dying, whilst the living had surrendered to lechery, drunkenness and looting; they were fleeing from a city with no moral values or rules, to retire to a 'stately palace, having a large and spacious court in the middest round engirt with galleries, halls, and chambers, every one separate alone by themselves, and beautified with pictures of admirable cunning. Nor was there any want of gardens, meadows, and other most pleasant walks, with wells and springs of fair running waters, all encompassed with branching vines, fitter for curious and quaffing bibbers, than women sober, and singularly modest.' Boccaccio wrote in 'The Induction' that 'they used delicate viands and excellent wines, avoiding luxury', and went on to describe something to the same effect at the beginning of every single day, clearly indicating that wine was an important element of a desired harmony, of a coveted ideal new world.

The story of Cistio the baker (Sixth Day, Second Tale), who through his wine and wit won the respect of Messer Geri Spina, a trusted friend of Pope Boniface, is quite remarkable. Although this story is neither the most popular, nor the most typical in *The Decameron*, it is particularly meaningful in the context of our topic; therefore, it is worth retelling in some detail.

Cistio the baker, who was a 'noble soul' but had apparently been neglected by Fortune, practised with dignity his not particularly prestigious trade. 'Now although Fortune had humbled him to so mean a condition, yet she added a blessing of wealth to that contemptible quality, and (as smiling on him continually) no disasters at any time befell him, but still he flourished in riches, lived like a jolly citizen, with all things fitting for honest entertainment about him, and plenty of the best wines (both white and claret) as Florence, or any part thereabout yielded.' Then one day Pope Boniface sent over several gentlemen of his court to conduct some very important business and they took lodgings at the house of Cistio's fellow

The Bean King, ***Jacob Jordaens***

Page 53: **The Fountain of Youth,** ***Italian miniature, fifteenth century***

townsman, Messer Geri. Every day they would walk past the baker's house, and he decided, as a matter of courtesy, to offer them a taste of his white wine. 'But having respect to his own mean degree, and the condition of Messer Geri, he thought it far unfitting for him to be so forward in such presumption; but rather entered into consideration of some such means, whereby Messer Geri might be the inviter of himself to taste his wine.' That is why at such times as Messer Geri and the papal ambassadors were due to pass by, Cistio would set before his door a tin pail of fresh chilled water, a small Bolognese clay vessel, full of his choicest white wine, and two small tin beakers, which were so thoroughly polished that they shone like silver. 'Down he sat, with all this provision before him, and emptying his stomach twice or thrice, of some clotted flegmes which seemed to offend it, even as the Gentlemen were passing by, he drank one or two rouses of his wine so heartily, and with such a pleasing appetite, as might have moved a longing almost in a dead man.'

On the third day Messer Geri could no longer resist the temptation and invited himself, and his guests, to try the wine. The baker personally seated and served them, but before that, when they commanded their servants to wash the cups, he told them: 'Fellows, now get you gone, and leave me to the performance of this service; for I am no worse a skinker than a baker, and tarry you never so long, you shall not drink a drop.' From then on, the company would stop by for a drink every day. When their affairs were concluded, Messer Geri prepared a very sumptuous feast for them 'inviting thereto the most part of the honourablest citizens, and Cistio to be one amongst them; who by no means would be seen in an assembly of such state and pomp, albeit he was most earnestly entreated'. When he heard that, Messer Geri sent one of his servants to bring back a small bottle of Cistio's wine in order 'to serve it in such sparing manner to the table, that each gentleman might be allowed half a glassful at their down-sitting'. The servant, apparently offended by the baker's words a few days earlier, decided to trick Cistio and brought with him a huge bottle, but the clever baker turned him back, telling him that Messer Geri had probably sent him to the river and not to Cistio. The silly servant reported to his master what the baker had told him word for word, and Messer Geri asked to see the bottle which the servant had taken to Cistio. He then sent the servant back, this time with a smaller bottle, which the good baker filled up. After the feast Cistio sent a cask of his wine to Messer Geri, and then went to his house in person and told him: 'Sir, I would not have you to imagine that the huge flaggon which first came did any jot dismay me; but rather I conceived that the small vial whereof you tasted every morning, yet filled many mannerly glasses together, was fallen quite out of your remembrance; in plainer terms, it being no wine for grooms or peasants, as yourself affirmed yesterday. And because I mean to be a skinker no longer, by keeping wine to please any other palate but mine own, I have sent you half my store, and hereafter think of me as you shall please.' Messer Geri realised what the baker had been trying to tell him all along and thanked him, 'accepting him always after as his intimate friend'.

That was how wine and, more specifically, the attitude to wine reduced the social gap between the gentleman and the baker. In a delicate but resolute manner, Cistio succeeded in drawing Messer Geri into the orbit of his ethical concept of wine and making him accept it. The implications are clear: the honour of drinking good wine is the preserve of those who bear their fate honourably. Good wine is a characteristic attribute of honour, irrespective of whether one is a nobleman or a tradesman. Honour and nobility, as Boccaccio frequently implied, are not exclusive to either noblemen or commoners. This condition of the soul, as this story elegantly proves, is reflected in one's attitude to wine.

Geoffrey Chaucer

Geoffrey Chaucer's Thirsty Pilgrims

According to a document of 1399, a year before his death Geoffrey Chaucer was granted by King Henry IV a generous annuity of £20 and a cask of 300 litres of wine.

It is not known whether Chaucer asked for this in-kind annuity himself, nor is it known whether he had met Boccaccio when he visited Florence in 1372; what we do know is that he must have been intimately acquainted with the world of wine (his father was an influential London vintner); this is quite obvious in his *Canterbury Tales*. In this work, wine is not simply a detail but often a building block in the portrayal of characters, sometimes playing an important part in the climax and denouement of the story. Describing each of the pilgrims, who engage in a storytelling contest while travelling together to Canterbury and back, Chaucer did not forget to include their eating and drinking habits in greater or lesser detail. The group included people from many walks of life: a knight, a prioress, a monk, a merchant, a lawyer, a franklin (landowner), a scholar, a miller, a reeve (steward of an estate), a pardoner; a wife of Bath and many others – 29 in all, in addition to Chaucer himself. Their dialogues and revealing confessions outline a fascinating portrait of fourteenth-century mores, in which wine and ale figure prominently. Most of the characters turn out to be if not heavy then at least habitual drinkers. The Franklin is a sanguine, white-bearded epicure, who is contended with life and loves all the pleasures of life, starting with wine:

Well lov'd he in the morn a sop in wine.
To liven in delight was ever his wont
*For he was Epicurus' own son.**

The Summoner, who would suffer 'for a quart of wine, a good fellow to have his concubine a twelvemonth, and excuse him at the full', is a common, semiliterate scoundrel, who obviously has a drink problem:

Well lov'd he garlic, onions, and leeks,
And for to drink strong wine as red as blood.
Then would he speak, and cry as he were wood;
And when that he well drunken had the wine,
Then would he speak no word but Latin.

Having suggested the idea of the storytelling contest and agreed to be its judge and to 'set a supper at a certain price', the Host (innkeeper) swears the following oath before he asks the pilgrims to draw lots in order to choose the first storyteller:

As ever may I drink wine or ale,
Whoso is rebel to my judgement,
Shall pay for all that by the way is spent.

The Wife of Bath swears the same oath before proceeding to tell the amusing tale of her five husbands: 'As ever may I drink wine or ale I shall say sooth', and later expounds her views on wine:

Metellius, the foul churl, the swine,
That with a staff bereft his wife of life
For she drank wine, though I had been his wife,
Never should he have daunted me from drink:
And, after wine, of Venus most I think.

**All quotes from* The Canterbury Tales *edited by D. Laing Purves*

The Shipman is also a drunkard and in his tale mentions wines from foreign lands: malvesie, or Malmesy wine, which derived its name from Malvasia, a region of the Morea near Cape Malea, where it was made; and vernage, or Vernaccia from Italy. The moral judgement passed on heavy drinking in 'The Pardoner's Tale' reveals a suspicious intimacy with the subject. In other words, the characters in *The Canterbury Tales* follow the pattern already established by Boccaccio. Wine makes their portrayals even more vivid and full-blooded, while their passion for wine implies an acute thirst for life.

Gargantua and Pantagruel's Monumental Drinking Bouts

If the pleasures of the flesh ultimately prevail over wine in Boccaccio's *Decameron*, the pleasures of the table undoubtedly dominate Rabelais's *Gargantua and Pantagruel* – the presence of food and wine in the book is nothing short of monumental. Rabelais quoted the motto *Hic bibitur* ('They drink here') at the beginning of *Gargantua and Pantagruel*, and remained faithful to it to the very last page. *Ventrem omnipotentem* (the omnipotent stomach) dominates the entire story. For Rabelais's characters, food and, to an even larger extent, drink are a way of learning about and attaining the world. The two giants Gargantua and Pantagruel have an enormous thirst and capacity for both sensual pleasures in the form of all kinds of food and drink, and for nobility and worldly wisdom. This is implied even by their names. Pantagruel means 'all-thirsty', from 'panta' ('all' in Greek) and 'gruel' ('thirsty' in the Hagarene language). Gargantua was thus named by his father Grangousier ('great throat' in French) because, as soon as he was born, he cried out with a high, sturdy and big voice, 'Some drink,

François Rabelais

some drink, some drink.'* Upon hearing this, the happy father exclaimed: 'How great and nimble a throat thou hast', and the son was called Gargantua because it was the first word that his father had spoken after his birth.

The sumptuous victuals arranged like a cavalcade, often covering whole pages, are invariably washed down lavishly with white, rosé and red wine from various parts of France.

The food and wine in the feast scenes make the characters of this phantasmagoria life-like and realistic. It is worth noting that Rabelais, who parodies everything around him – science, the law, government, the Church and religion – treats food with reverence and deference, and wine, in particular, almost with veneration. In the words of Bacbuc, the High Priestess of the Holy Bottle: '[H]ere we hold not that laughing, but that drinking is the distinguishing character of man. I don't say drinking, taking that word singly and absolutely in the strictest sense; no, beasts then might put in for a share; I mean drinking cool delicious wine. For you must know, my beloved, that by wine we become divine; neither can there be a surer argument or a less deceitful divination.'

In his Prologue to the Third Book, Rabelais addressed his readers: 'Good people, most illustrious drinkers, and you, thrice precious gouty gentlemen … you are not young, which is a competent quality for you to philosophate more than physically in wine, not in vain, and henceforwards to be of the Bacchic Council; to the end that, opining there, you may give your opinion faithfully of the substance, colour, excellent odour, eminency, propriety, faculty, virtue, and effectual dignity of the said blessed and desired liquor.' These words prove beyond doubt that we can find a true oenologist in the sixteenth century.

'I never drink without thirst, either present or future. To prevent it, as you know, I drink for the thirst to come. I drink eternally. This is to me an eternity of drinking, and drinking of eternity,' Grangousier explains. 'O companion! if I could mount up as well as I can get [wine] down [my throat], I had been long ere this above the sphere of the moon with Empedocles,' the cunning and witty Panurge says. When the storyline proves too limited to accommodate all outbursts of gastronomic ecstasy, the author inserts parody titles of imaginary books, such as *The Prickle of Wine*, *The Spur of Cheese*, *Of Peas and Bacon, cum Commento*, *The Teeth-chatter or Gum-didder of Lubberly Lusks*, *The Hotchpot of Hypocrites*, *The Bibbings of the Tippling Bishops*, and many others in the same vein.

---

* *All quotes from* Gargantua and Pantagruel *translated by Sir Thomas Urquhart of Cromarty and Peter Antony Motteux*

Let us stop here because, as a leading satirical character in nineteenth-century Russia put it, 'No one can fathom the unfathomable' – a maxim that is entirely true with respect to the reincarnations of wine in Rabelais's works.

William Shakespeare: Sherry Lover, Beer Sceptic?

William Shakespeare

Although in Shakespeare's works the passions seem slightly more exalted, the pleasures of the table are not totally ignored. Asked if he thinks that life consists of the four elements, Sir Andrew in *Twelfth Night* replies, 'Faith, so they say; but I think it rather consists of eating and drinking', having admitted earlier to being 'a great eater of beef' even though he believes it is harmful to his wit. It seems reasonable to assume that the Bard might have been expressing his own views on food and, particularly, on wine when he created Sir John Falstaff, the larger than life character in *Henry IV*. Gluttonous, adventurous, deceitful, physically huge, stunningly amoral and outrageously funny, Falstaff is one of the few characters without a clear historical prototype; therefore, it is quite likely that Shakespeare might have attributed to him some of his personal ideas about the pleasures of life. Sir John loved them so dearly that he was said to have sold his soul to the devil on Good Friday for a cup of Madeira and a cold capon's leg.

Falstaff has a cogent theory about the relationship between intellectual development and the table. In his view, people who prefer 'thin drink' to wine have no sense of humour. But most fascinating of all is his monologue on sherry (see p. 62). In addition to a good knowledge of alcohol and human nature, this revealing monologue implies the author's desire to share some of his most intimate thoughts with the world. Thus, to the many mysteries surrounding William Shakespeare's personality, one might add the hypothesis that he was very partial to strong Spanish wines and, moreover, had a condescending and somewhat sceptical attitude to beer. This conclusion is supported by various allusions in Shakespeare's plays. We will quote a single line from *Henry IV, Part II*, where Prince Hal admits that he would like some 'small beer' and Poins, a confidant and boon companion of the prince, tells him: 'Why, a prince should not be so loosely studied, as to remember so weak a composition.'

The Melancholic Wine of the Orient

Someone might object that our reflections on the ethics and aesthetics of wine have so far been too Eurocentric, and proceed to quote Omar Khayyám. Such an objection would hardly have anything but purely geographical grounds. The entire oeuvre of this Persian poet (1048–1131) was imbued with a spirit of revolt against the emergence of an 'anti-wine' culture, and has a poignancy unique to the transitional age in which he lived. It would be sufficient to quote one of the many verses that show Omar's heartfelt opposition to the prohibition of what he considered natural, beautiful and humane:

Omar Khayyám

Why, be this Juice the growth of God, who dare
Blaspheme the twisted tendril as a Snare?
A Blessing, we should use it, should we not?
*And if a Curse – why, then, Who set it there?**

The recurrent themes of love and wine have made Omar's poetry forever modern, topical and frequently quoted by winemakers, who want to embellish their advertisements with a short, beautiful, profound, and classic passage.

It should be noted that Omar's attitude to wine was not unique in mediaeval Irano-Persian poetry. Wine figured prominently not only as a detail but also and much more often as an object of sincere and sensuous admiration and veneration in the works of the greatest poets from the age of the Iranian Renaissance (tenth–fifteenth century) – Rudaki, Sadi, Ferdowsi, Nezami and Ali Shir Nava'i. It would be difficult to speculate what fruits this originally wine-loving culture would have yielded if it had been given the historical chance to follow its own logic and path of development. What we know for sure is that it was imbued with humanism, and this made it interesting and, even more importantly, understandable to the Europeans of the nineteenth century, when these poets gradually became known in Europe.

Before we end this chapter, let us go back to what was said at the beginning. The spiritual pulse of European culture is attuned to and reflected in wine. This applies not only to antiquity and the Renaissance. During the age of Romanticism in the nineteenth century, wine appeared in a new guise – self-reflective and rich in psychological associations, in line with an emerging new aesthetic. As an illustration, it is sufficient to quote the reflections of the conductor Johannes Kreisler in Hoffmann's *Fantasy Pieces in the Style of Callot*: 'The conscientious musician who wants to compose an operetta must

* *All quotes from* The Rubáiyát of Omar Khayyám *translated by Edward FitzGerald.*

The Marriage at Cana ***(fragment), Giotto***

drink champagne. In it he will find the playful and light gaiety necessary for the genre. Religious music requires Rhine or Jurançon wine. In them, as in all deep thoughts, there is an intoxicating bitterness, but the composition of heroic music requires Burgundy; in it there is power and patriotic fervour.' Let us also recall Baudelaire's memorable dictum: 'A man who drinks nothing but water has something to hide from his close ones.'

In conclusion, we should like to point out that when analysing the revolutionary changes in life in every period of human history, along with events such as the invention of gunpowder or double-entry bookkeeping; the great geographical discoveries; the introduction of potatoes, maize and tobacco to Europe; or the invention of the steam engine, one should not ignore the state of winemaking and the attitude to wine, because they have always mirrored people's attitudes.

Tapestry (fragment), fifteenth century

Persian miniature, fourteenth century

Hedylus, Greek poet (third century BC)

Let us drink, then
And
perhaps we'll find
something new
in our wine –

some eloquent, honey-coloured word.

So come!
Fill me up with jugs of Chian wine and say,
'Go ahead, Hedylus, play!'

I hate an empty life –
empty of wine. *

Monologue of Falstaff on the Glorious Dry Sherris

A good sherris-sack hath a two-fold operation in it. It ascends me into the brain; dries me there all the foolish and dull and crudy vapours which environ it; makes it apprehensive, quick, forgetive, full of nimble, fiery, and delectable shapes; which delivered o're to the voice, the tongue, which is the birth, becomes excellent wit. The second property of your excellent sherris is the warming of the blood; which before, cold and settled, left the liver white and pale; which is the badge of pusillanimity and cowardice; but the sherris warms it, and makes it course from the inwards to the parts extremes. It illumineth the face, which, as a beacon, gives warning to all the rest of this little kingdom, man, to arm; and then the vital commoners and inland petty spirits muster me all to their captain, the heart, who, great and puff'd up with this retinue, doth any deed of courage – and this valour comes of sherris. So that skill in the weapon is nothing without sack, for that sets it a-work; and learning, a mere hoard of gold kept by a devil till sack commences it and sets it in act and use. Hereof comes it that Prince Harry is valiant; for the cold blood he did naturally inherit of his father, he hath, like lean, sterile, and bare land, manured, husbanded, and till'ed, with excellent endeavour of drinking good and good store of fertile sherris, that he is become very hot and valiant. If I had a thousand sons, the first humane principle I would teach them should be to forswear thin potations, and to addict themselves to sack.

From *King Henry IV, Part II*,
by William Shakespeare

From The Prologue to *The Canterbury Tales*

A Franklin was in this company;
White was his beard, as is the daisy.
Of his complexion he was sanguine.
Well lov'd he in the morn a sop in wine.
To liven in delight was ever his wont,
For he was Epicurus' own son,
That held opinion, that plein delight
Was verily felicity perfite.
An householder, and that a great, was he;
Saint Julian** he was in his country.
His bread, his ale, was alway after one;
A better envined man was nowhere none;
Without bake-meat never was his house,
Of fish and flesh, and that so plenteous,
It snowed in his house of meat and drink,
Of all dainties that men could think.
After the sundry seasons of the year,
So changed he his meat and his supper.
Full many a fat partridge had he in mew,
And many a bream, and many a luce in stew
Woe was his cook, but if his sauce were
Poignant and sharp, and ready all his gear.
His table dormant in his hall alway
Stood ready cover'd all the long day.

* *Translated by George Theodorides*

***St Julian: The patron saint of hospitality, celebrated for supplying his votaries with good lodging and good cheer*

Vinaria

From *The Rubáiyát of Omar Khayyám*

A Book of Verses underneath the Bough,
A Jug of Wine, a Loaf of Bread – and Thou
Beside me singing in the Wilderness –
Oh, Wilderness were Paradise enow!

* * *

Perplext no more with Human or Divine,
To-morrow's tangle to the winds resign,
And lose your fingers in the tresses of
The Cypress-slender Minister of Wine.

* * *

Waste not your Hour, nor in the vain pursuit
Of This and That endeavor and dispute;
Better be jocund with the fruitful Grape
Than sadden after none, or bitter, Fruit.

You know, my Friends, with what a brave Carouse I
made a Second Marriage in my house;
Divorced old barren Reason from my Bed,
And took the Daughter of the Vine to Spouse.

For 'Is' and 'Is-not' though with Rule and Line
And 'UP-AND-DOWN' by Logic I define,
Of all that one should care to fathom, I
was never deep in anything but – Wine.

chapter 3

A Vinocentric Review of Bulgarian History

In Bulgaria, it is rare for Bulgarians not to have vineyards. This is their favourite occupation. A peasant considers himself unhappy and feels ashamed if he does not have a vineyard.

G. S. Rakovski, *Introduction* (1859)

Scene from The Apocalypse, fresco by Dimitar Zograph in the narthex of the Church of the Nativity of the Virgin, Rila Monastery, Bulgaria, 1847

Thracian Wine at the Gates of Troy

Bulgaria holds quite a special place in the European history of wine. Most ancient authors after Homer believed that the cult of the merry god of wine Dionysus originated in ancient Thrace, from where it eventually spread throughout the Hellenistic world – an assumption that must have remained unchallenged for a long time (around a thousand years), considering that Pliny the Elder (first century AD) claimed that the first vine-grower in Europe was the Thracian Eumolpus.

Wine is a very important element of the image of the ancient Thracians. The Homeric epics depict them as brave and handsome men who fight on chariots richly decorated with gold and silver, carry 'weapons of gold, huge and wondrous', and ride horses 'as fleet as the blasts of the wind', and who also make and drink fine wine in beautiful cups. In this period, at the end of the second millennium BC, the Thracians were at the zenith of their power and glory. As part of the large 'Palaeobalkan-Western Asia Minor' community, the Thracians undoubtedly played a significant role in the formation of ancient Greek culture – not only through the cult of Dionysus but also through the cults of Orpheus and Ares, which are of Thracian origin too. We must keep in mind that in the time of Herodotus (fifth century BC), 'Europe' meant Greece, Thrace and Macedonia.

Homer's *Iliad* refers to the 'honey-sweet black wine, which the ships of the Achaeans brought daily from the Thracian city of Ismarus to their camp outside Troy. The *Odyssey* describes 'the dark wine and sweet' of Maron, king of the Cicones. The cunning hero from Ithaca used precisely this wine to get Polyphemus the Cyclops drunk before blinding him. 'By spear my Ismaric wine is won, which I drink, leaning upon my spear', the Greek poet Archilochus (seventh century BC) writes in one of his elegies. In his *Works and Days*, Hesiod mentions 'wine of Biblis', which, according to some ancient authors, meant Thracian wine.

The works of later Greek writers portray the Thracians as insufferable drunkards – an image that has survived to the present day. Unlike the civilised Greeks, the Thracians drank their wine undiluted with water, and this manner of drinking was called 'Scythian', that is, barbarian. The Greek historian Theopompus (fourth century BC) tells how Kotys I (383–359 BC), the king of the Odryssae (a Thracian tribe that lived on what is modern Bul-

Dionysian scene on silver jug, Thracian treasure from the village of Borovo near Rousse, Bulgaria, fourth century BC

Grape Crushing, ***scene from a Thracian bas-relief found near Assenovgrad, Bulgaria***

garian territory), once got hideously drunk and lay in bed waiting for the goddess Athena to join him. After a little while he got up and asked one of his guards if the goddess was coming, to which the man foolishly replied that she was not whereupon he was killed on the spot. The next guard to be asked told Kotys that Athena would come any minute, and this saved his life. Xenophon describes a feast at the court of the Odryssian king Seuthes I (424–410 BC), who would drink wine from a horn and then pour the rest over his clothes. The writer was impressed that despite the huge amount of wine which he had drunk the Thracian chief remained apparently sober. Some Greek writers claimed that the Thracians would share everything except for two things: their sword and their cup.

For the Thracians, wine was a sacred element of religious practice. Through it, they became one with the gods; therefore, they might have preferred their wine thick, sweet and strong because they wanted to achieve this state faster – in other words, what the ancient writers considered barbarian behaviour might have been related to this characteristic Thracian religious and cultural tradition. 'Considering the special ritual value of wine in ancient Thrace, it becomes clear why so many precious vessels have been found on Thracian lands', Prof. Ivan Marazov notes (*The Thracians and Wine*, Sofia, 2000). More than 180 gold *phialae* (wine cups), or more than half of those discovered in the whole ancient world, were found on Thracian territory. Many of them are decorated with the figure of the merry god of wine Dionysus. This no doubt highly developed wine culture is represented by many other archaeological monuments: votive plates, bas-reliefs, and vessels and coins decorated with vine and wine motifs have been found all over Bulgaria. It seems that the cultivation of some of

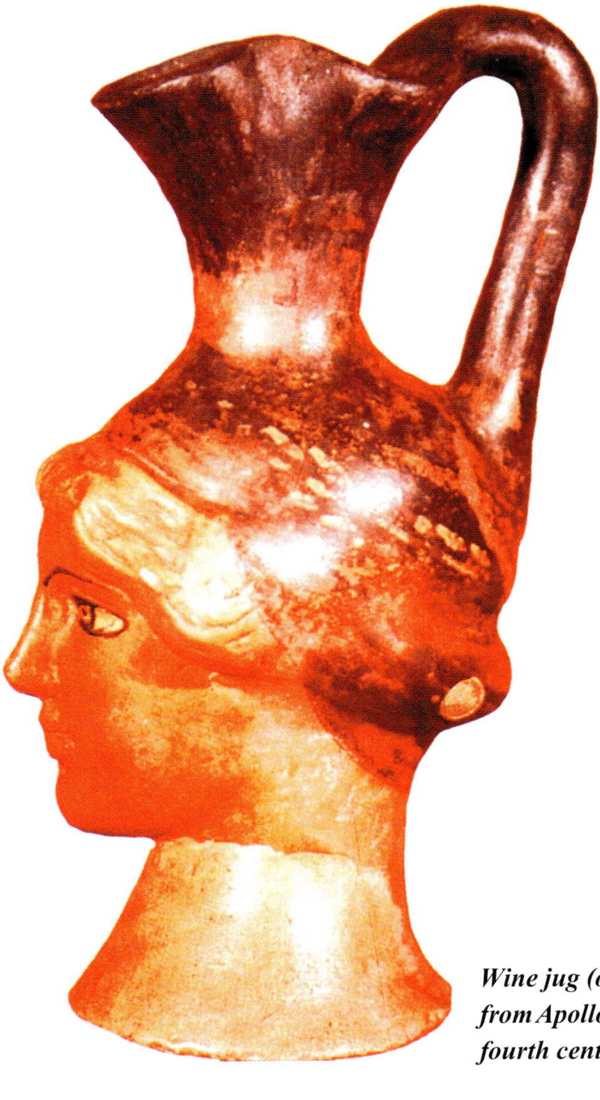

Wine jug (oinochoe) from Apollonia, fourth century BC

Silver coin of the Thracian king Saratokos

Amphora from Apollonia (Sozopol), Bulgaria, fifth century BC

Page 70–71: Scene from the cupola of the Thracian tomb near Kazanlak, Bulgaria, fourth century BC

the oldest native varieties – such as Pamid, Red Misket, Dimiat, Gamza, Mavrud and Broad Vine of Melnik – dates back to Thracian times.

Today we can only guess what those wines must have tasted like. They were probably quite sweet and aromatic. At least that is how ancient writers describe them: 'When he drank [this sweet wine, unblended, and of the most exquisite flavour], he mixed twenty parts of water to one of wine, and yet the fragrance from the mixing-bowl was so exquisite that it was impossible to refrain from drinking' (*Odyssey*, Book IX, 208–210). The wine of the Thracian king Maron, which Odysseus praises so highly, must have been quite thicker and stronger than other wines in the ancient world, where mixing one part of wine to four parts of water was common practice.

The Roman conquest of the Balkan peninsula did not stop the development of winemaking. According to some sources, cultivation of white varieties increased in the Roman period, particularly in the eastern part and along the Black Sea coast. Perhaps the vineyards that Ovid saw near Anchialo (Pomorie) and Messembria (Nessebar) on his way to exile in Tomi in AD 8 were of white grape varieties.

Thracian treasure (wine-drinking set)
from the village of Borovo near Rousse, Bulgaria,
fourth century BC

Amphora and rhyton
from the Panagyurishte
Gold Treasure,
fourth century BC

The Wine of Mediaeval Bulgarians

The ancient vine-growing and winemaking tradition, which the Slavs and Bulgars found among the Romanised and Hellenised Thracian population when they settled in the Balkans in the sixth and seventh centuries, was integrated naturally into the life of mediaeval Bulgaria. The traditional story of how the Bulgarian khan Krum (ninth century) had supposedly uprooted all vineyards on Bulgarian territory is not true. Its only source is a mediaeval Byzantine encyclopaedia (*Suidas*) and is not corroborated by other evidence. At the same time, the famous *Anonymus Vaticanus* recounts how the soldiers of Nicephorus I, who seized Krum's palaces, 'found his cellars full' and were allowed by the Byzantine emperor to drink as much wine as they wanted. Considering that this was in July 811, the khan and his retinue must have been so accustomed to wine that they did not want to risk running out of supplies before the new crop. It could be that precisely this violation made Krum even thirstier for revenge. Looting the royal wine cellar is not an act of common looting but of humiliation of the ruler, because it violates one of his most intimate spaces. This makes it somehow easier to understand why, after he routed the Byzantine army at the Varbitsa pass and captured the emperor himself, Khan Krum killed Nicephorus, had his skull encrusted in silver and used it as a drinking goblet with which he toasted his guests.

Bulgaria's conversion to Christianity in 864 gave a new impetus to local viticulture for entirely obvious reasons. The development of vine-growing was encouraged by the state. Throughout the period from the ninth to the end of the fourteenth century, wine is mentioned in historical sources as an invariable sign of prosperity. The *Anonymous Bulgarian Chronicle* (eleventh century) refers to 'an abundance of everything – that is, wheat and butter, milk and wine' in the time of Tsar Peter (927–969). In Bulgaria, as in Western Europe, the Church tried to impose some moderation in wine drinking. 'Do not bury your talent in food, do not hide God's pearl in drunkenness,' Presbyter Kozma (an eminent Bulgarian theologian, writer and cleric from the tenth century) advises, at the same time condemning 'the vile heretics who command us to abstain totally from both meat and wine, considering them to be foul'. Similar criticisms of excessive drinking can be found in John the Exarch's *Hexameron*.

By the ninth century, wine had become an administrative problem for the Bulgarian empire. Every subject who owned a pair of oxen had to pay a tax of one modius of wheat and one jug of wine. Wine was also part of the Church tax *canonicon*. The farm law referred to 'wine from a jar, cask, and vat', and had no fewer than twelve provisions regulating matters related to viticulture and winemaking. Their importance in the life of mediaeval Bulgarians is obvious from Article 59 of the law, which stipulates the following: 'Whoever cuts or uproots other people's vines shall have his hand chopped off shall be fined.' Those who were caught stealing from vineyards were punished by being 'beaten and stripped of their clothes'. The records mention wine as part of the subsistence level on a par with wheat. The law prescribes the same punishment for stealing wine as for stealing wheat. In the royal charters the words 'vineyards', 'winemakers' and 'wine' are used as frequently as 'fields' and 'wheat growers'. A miniature in the Gospels (Tetraevangelia) of Tsar Ivan Alexander (1331–1371) depicts a scene in which vines are pruned with a vine-hook. The choice of this particular scene as an illustration in the royal copy of the

Page 75: Khan Krum celebrates victory over Emperor Nicephorus, miniature from the Bulgarian translation of the* Chronicle *of Manasses

Gospels is a clear indication of the importance of viticulture in the empire. The ritual significance of wine at the royal and noble tables is also well documented. It can be inferred from the inscription on a beautiful gilded silver cup from Shumen, 'Bless fifty times he who drinks' (written in Cyrillic characters), and that on a fourteenth-century ring, 'Cupbearer Peter, cousin to the tsar'. The *Synodicon* of the Bulgarian Church (thirteenth century) refers to one 'Monk Silvester, who was cupbearer to the great Tsar Ivan Asen'.

The evidence of the quality of mediaeval Bulgarian wine is conflicting, and varies from heartfelt confessions of love to utter disgust; by and large, however, positive opinions prevail. In one of his letters, Archbishop Theophylactus of Ohrid (early twelfth century) speaks warmly about 'the light and very subtle Ohrid wine'. During the same period, the Greek bishop Gregory of Antioch complains about 'the sour wine of the Bulgarians, revolting, unfermented and hazy in appearance, unpleasant in smell and bitter in taste', which he drank in Sredets (Sofia) and which in his opinion was 'like a pointed spear for the stomach'.

The men of the French knight Gofrois de Villardouaine, a participant in the Fourth Crusade, found excellent wine in Assenovgrad in 1205, as his diaries prove. According to a local legend, it was the quality of local wine that saved the town from being burnt by the crusaders. The Mavrud which they tried made them merciful, and they spared the town and its inhabitants. This story was recorded in a chronicle of the tavern-keepers' guild in the town, which has unfortunately been lost since.

There are also flattering accounts of local wine in the writings of other mediaeval West European travellers across the Bulgarian lands. Yet, the majority of these accounts were more impressed by the abundance, rather than the quality of Bulgarian wine.

An Italian document of 1366 notes that after pillaging the Bulgarian Black Sea coast and seizing the town of Nessebar, Count Amedeus of Savoy promptly ordered the sale of the soured wine that he found there and the purchase of fine wine from Anchialo (Pomorie). The market apparently allowed the quick and easy replacement of bad wines with better ones. In Bulgaria, as in Western Europe, the first creators of certain standards in wine production were several monasteries that traded in wine. The monastery of St George in Skopje had a special trading venue for wine, whilst, according to some studies, wines from Melnik and Plovdiv were traded across a comparatively large area in southeastern and central Europe in the thirteenth and fourteenth centuries. The busy trade with Dubrovnik during that period contributed significantly to their recognition.

A late eleventh-century *typikon* (a liturgical book which contains instructions about the order of the various church services and ceremonies) from Bachkovo monastery gives some idea of the quantities imbibed by mediaeval Bulgarians. According to the Bachkovo *typikon*, the daily ration of monks included four cups of wine, six in the days from Easter to Pentecost, and up to eight on special occasions. Archaeological studies on pottery from the period indicate that the size of cups varied from 180 to 230 millilitres, meaning that the daily ration approximated one litre or more.

The winepress was not used in Bulgaria during the Middle Ages. Wine was produced and stored in wooden casks and vats, but also in *pythoi* (large spherical earthenware jars) and jars (an anachronism that persisted stubbornly in some places to the very end of the nineteenth century). Accord-

The Last Supper ***and*** **The Parable of the Master and His Servants** ***(below), miniatures from The Gospels of Tsar Ivan Alexander, fourteenth century***

ing to the Hungarian ethnologist Istvan Vincze, author of several extensive studies on the development of vinification techniques, this means that most of the wines would have been tart, tannic reds and blacks produced by open fermentation of grapes. This assumption is corroborated by the wide and persistent use of wooden vats as an intermediate stage in the technological transition from earthenware vessels to wooden barrels, that is, from open (exposed to oxygen) to closed fermentation. The West European practice of maturing wines in underground cellars was not popular in Bulgaria. Wine was usually stored in *pythoi* and jars buried in the ground, according to a tradition inherited from antiquity and still preserved in the Caucasus (the so-called Kakhetian technique). That was precisely what the German Hans Dernschwam saw on his way to Constantinople in 1553. He noted in his diary: 'In the villages they do not have many casks or cellars. … People in the villages and in the towns keep wine in stone amphorae and draw it from them with a jug or measure until it finishes.'

The Parable of the Barren Fig Tree *and* **The Miracle at Cana in Galilee,** ***miniatures from The Gospels of Tsar Ivan Alexander, fourteenth century***

Silver cup inscribed as belonging to Sibin, grand zhupan (governor) of Bulgaria, ninth century

The Wine of Lost Liberty

Bulgaria was under Ottoman rule from the fifteenth to the nineteenth century, a period which – for two reasons – was virtually a disaster for winemaking. Islam encouraged neither winemaking nor drinking. The Bulgarian nobility was wiped out, and for centuries there was no one to set the tone in the quest for sophisticated pleasures, which undoubtedly include drinking fine wine. The fragile standards in winemaking, achieved in the thirteenth and fourteenth centuries, were soon forgotten. Still, albeit in conditions of semi-legality, winemaking and drinking remained an important ethnic marker of Christian communities in the Ottoman Empire. This specific function is clearly illustrated in the epic poems devoted to the folk hero Krali Marko, who often ate roasted lambs and barren cows and drank wine in a cool tavern or outdoors by the Aegean sea before or after performing his feats. One of the poems tells how Krali Marko went to Constantinople to look for his brother and, upon arriving in the city, stopped at a tavern, where he was offered coffee and sherbet. Marko replied:

I cannot drink coffee,
Nor can I drink sherbet.
Give me three-year-old wine,
For me and for my horse.

Another poem tells how Sultan Selim sent a Black Arab to kill Marko because he made janissaries drink wine during Ramadan. Wine drinking also appears as a symbol of manliness and prowess in the descriptions of Krali Marko's cup, which, according to different versions, could hold the equivalent of 15 to 110 litres.

Most of the evidence about the actual state of Bulgarian winemaking in the period comes from Western European diplomats, merchants, captives or simply adventurers who, for one reason or another, found themselves in European Turkey. The prevailing opinion of Bulgarian wine was not flattering, particularly from the fifteenth to the seventeenth century. Wine was hard to find and was usually of inferior quality. 'We could not obtain wine for three days, because, even though there was some in that poor village [Dragoman], according to local custom it is stored in goatskins, partly by the fire, and it is sour, so anyone would prefer to drink snow water rather than that wine,' Adam von Kleilsheim wrote in his travel notes (1616), adding that 'good wine can hardly be found from Belgrade to Constantinople'. There are, however, some radically different opinions. 'You would not believe that in the middle of Turkey we had a great

Bulgarian Peasants, ***drawing by H. Beck (1586), Austrian National Library, Vienna***

abundance of wine, which serves as a cure during bad nights,' writes the Frenchman Ogier de Busbecq (1553), going on to add that good wine could be found only in the places populated by Christians. The Hungarian traveller Tomas Borsos, who in May 1613 found himself in Nikopol, describes the local wines as 'extremely sweet and strong', while, in the description of his journey from Vienna to Constantinople in 1564, the Austrian Jacob Betzek mentions 'fine red wine', which an old Bulgarian sold to his companions and because of which they later received a severe beating from their otherwise kind host after they got drunk and started making passes at his daughter.

Similar brief notes have been left by numerous other travellers. Almost all of them have an occasion to mention Bulgarian wine, which they sometimes find to be too strong or too sweet, but nevertheless acceptable. It seems that during those centuries wine made Bulgarians somewhat more comprehensible – and, perhaps, closer – to Europeans. Apart from a vital necessity, wine was also a special envoy, a mediator between two already separate worlds.

The mid-eighteenth century saw a certain upturn in Bulgarian winemaking. The change may be attributed to the emergence of a more affluent class among the Ottoman Empire's Christian population, which gradually began to make and demand better quality wine. Output soared in this period, and wine was even exported. 'Bulgaria produces quite a large quantity of red wine, but of

poor quality. Every year 5,000 to 6,000 carts arrive from Russia and Poland to load those wines,' the French diplomat Charles de Peyssonnel noted in his *Traité sur le commerce de la Mer Noire*. His observations were made in the 1760s and 1770s, when he was consul in various Turkish cities, and they are corroborated by other authors.

One of the first compliments to Bulgarian winemaking was paid by the French doctor Paul Lucas. In 1706 he visited Stanimaka (Assenovgrad) and was strongly impressed by 'the local wine, which is splendid', as well as by the size of the casks and vats used by local winemakers. The scale of production clearly shows that the wine was designed for markets beyond Stanimaka, which would have entailed an effort to keep quality consistent and competitive. This also applies to the region of Melnik, which in the seventeenth and eighteenth centuries engaged in a lively trade with central Asia and, in particular, with Austria-Hungary. These contacts helped introduce new winemaking techniques and standards, according to the ethnologist Lili Peneva Vincze ('Central European Influences in the Emergence of Melnik Wine Cellars', in *Bulgarian Ethnography*, No. 1, 1984). She has in mind the distinctive tunnel-like cellars dug into the hills in the area, as well as some typical local wines. Those two new characteristics in Bulgaria have parallels in eastern Hungary and, in particular, the Tokaj region, whereas the records suggest that those parallels were the result of extensive trade contacts. In *Travels Along the Valleys of the Struma, Mesta and Bregalnitsa Rivers* (1894), the Bulgarian ethnologist Vassil Kanchov wrote that ordinary Melnik wines were sold in the same year they were produced, mainly in Nevrokop, Ser, Djoumaya and Kavala (southwestern Bulgaria), adding that 'in some houses they make excellent thick wines from dried grapes which last for many years and can easily rival the European wines of a similar kind'. It is quite likely that the recipe for those wines, which were made by a technique that apparently made them similar to Tokay wines, came from the Tokaj region. The influence may have been mutual, because, in the sixteenth century, the region around the town of Eger, known as a producer of white wines, started producing reds, too, which the local people called '*ratsko*', or 'Turkish', wine. Istvan Vincze thinks that this new fashion was brought to the region by southern Slavic immigrants.

National Revival Wine

More and more encouraging assessments of Bulgarian wine appeared after the beginning of the nineteenth century. Particularly valuable evidence is provided by the Frenchman P. Seiget, who in 1829 travelled across eastern Bulgaria in search of archaeological sites and, among other things, sampled local wine. He found that wine around Malko Turnovo was 'quite good', and that around Lozengrad there was 'good quality red, which is very much like Petit Bourgogne'; he had 'fine red' near Topolovgrad and 'bad local wine' in Burgas. Wine around Yambol was of 'low quality', but the neighbouring town of Sliven produced 'lots of wine of excellent quality'. The Frenchman noted that around Karnobat there was 'little wine of poor quality', and in Anchialo, there was 'good-quality white, very much like the wine from Grave'. Those fleeting parallels between Bulgarian and French wine – made by a Frenchman – are music to the ears of Bulgarians even today. Sliven wines were also praised by the renowned Hungarian ethnologist Felix Kanitz, who travelled through the Bulgarian lands in the 1870s. He thought that 'Sliven wines are to Bulgaria what Tokay wine is to the Hungarians'. Whereas the Englishman James Baker, the author of the remarkable book *Turkey in Europe*, which was published in London in 1877 and received with huge interest throughout Western Europe, wrote that Sliven wines are 'excellent and similar to red Burgundy'.

Grape Harvest in the Western Balkans,
Austrian drawing, nineteenth century

Many of the Bulgarian National Revival activists felt compelled to pronounce on local wine. Georgi S. Rakovski (1821–1867), the ideologue of the Bulgarian national revolution, describes in his book *Introduction* (1859) local vine-growing and winemaking in minutest detail – from the choice of suitable canes and places for planting ('usually in sunny spots') to the technique of making wine and distilling *rakiya*, the Bulgarian equivalent of Italian grappa. He lists eighteen black and white grape varieties, including Gamza, Red Misket and Pamid, by their local names. Some of them

P. R. Slaveykov

G. S. Rakovski

L. Karavelov

are sweet, but others disappeared from Bulgarian vineyards after the arrival of phylloxera.

'A peasant considers himself unhappy and feels ashamed if he does not have a vineyard', Rakovski wrote, adding that even the Bulgarians who emigrated to Bessarabia planted vineyards immediately after settling down, even though the climate was not suitable for vine-growing. The grape harvest was a time of 'great merriment in villages and towns, with everyone busy and eager to collect the fruits of his labour and to make wine that will bring him joy all year long'. Rakovski stressed that 'Bulgarians do not use any tricks at all in their winemaking, such as boiling wines and mixing them with various toxic substances, but when they make it, they wait for it to froth [that is, ferment] of itself, rack it once and leave it over the winter, and then in spring they rack it once again, draining it off into other, clean casks or back into the same ones after they have cleaned them and removed the mud [that is, marc] from which they make palinka [*rakiya*].' Although the available knowledge and skills generally did not allow production of wine that could be aged, the author did not omit to note that 'in some towns winemaking is sufficiently advanced and one can also find excellent old wine made 15 or 20 years ago'. He also mentioned artificial halting of fermentation by adding 'white earth or embers' so that the wine would remain 'forever sweet'. The ideologue of the Bulgarian National Revival obviously believed firmly that a nation that could make good wine deserved national independence and would gain it eventually 'by a moral revolution and by force of arms'.

A similar understanding of the role of wine in the national awakening must have motivated also the teacher, poet, journalist and politician of the National Revival, Petko Rachov Slaveykov (1827–1895), who in 1870 published the first Bulgarian cookbook: *A Cookbook or Instructions About All Kinds of Dishes as They Are Prepared in Constantinople*. The section on 'Assorted Beverages' provided quite detailed information and recipes for making mead, beer, fruit wines and *rakiya*. It described in detail the entire production cycle of cider, noting that this variety of apple wine was made in France and Britain. Although hardly any Bulgarian would have rushed to experiment with cider, Slaveykov obviously thought it important that his readers should know what kind of wine other nations drank and how it was made. Perhaps this was also the reason that he included a recipe for 'artificial wine that has become popular in France'. By that time, phylloxera had already spread in Western Europe, and the French were producing counterfeit wines on a large scale.

Since Bulgarian wine vocabulary was still poor at the time, Slaveykov introduced terms such as 'spirit frothing' (*spirtovno shoupvanie*) 'sour frothing' (*kiselo shoupvanie*) and 'rotten frothing' (*gnilo shoupvanie*) in explaining the different stages of fermentation. He devoted a special chapter to good wine, offering helpful advice and tips on how to

Old Testament scene from the altar of the Church of the Holy Virgin, Pazardjik, Bulgaria, mid-nineteenth century

Wooden vessel for grape transportation (foutiya)

make it, when to rack it, how to prevent souring, and how to restore spoiled wine. 'Wine can indeed be made from various fruits and in various ways, but the purest and best wine is always made from grapes,' Slaveykov wrote, proceeding to list several basic rules of winemaking: pick the grapes when they are perfectly ripe, work in clean rooms and use clean vessels, separate white from black grapes, and so on. In addition, he recommends that ripe and unripe grapes should not be mixed but, rather, crushed and made into wine separately. From unripe grapes, 'You can also make wine that is light and tart, but you must drink it earlier because it does not last, whilst when you crush and mix ripe and unripe grapes you deny yourself the advantage of having prime quality fine and durable wine,' the old enlightener advised. Strange as it might sound, Slaveykov dealt with winemaking matters for the same reason that, before Bulgaria's liberation in 1878 from Ottoman rule, he published

Wooden wine vessel (baklitsa)

a magazine and two newspapers, wrote poetry and satire, worked as a teacher, and participated in the struggle for ecclesiastical independence. In 1863, when he started publishing his first newspaper, he defined its purpose as 'the awakening of the Bulgarians' and printed this epithet under the heading. Awakening the Bulgarians was his mission in life, and this required not only educational and political awakening but also a new way of life.

A publisher from Samokov, Dimitar Smrikarov, also contributed to the development of a new attitude to wine during the National Revival. In 1870 Smrikarov published in Belgrade a book that was quite popular at the time, *The Golden Source*, a collection of domestic, farming and health tips, originally published in England, that was translated into many European languages, which included instructions on vine and wine issues. Smrikarov must have found them somewhat inadequate, because four years later he published *Supplements to the Golden Source*, in which he gave priority to his studies on winemaking, diligently collected for many years, which in his view were superior in 'importance and originality' to those in *The Golden Source*. The contribution of another publisher, Hristo G. Danov, is also noteworthy. He published a calendar of the annual cycle *Yearflow*, which included practical advice and tips on vine-growing and winemaking.

National Revival interest in winemaking reached its zenith in 1873, when Grigor Nachovich published in Vienna the first Bulgarian *Manual of Winemaking*. At that time, Nachovich, who would become a minister after Bulgaria regained its independence in 1878, was studying economics and political science in the Austrian capital. Like Rakovski and Slaveykov, he believed that national independence must not find Bulgarians without modern knowledge of winemaking; therefore, he compiled a manual from French and German sources. The manual was quite advanced for its day and included detailed instructions on choosing the location of a vineyard, planting and fertilisation, as well as invaluable technical advice on how to separate the juice from the grape skins and stems. Nachovich's thoughts on the role of oxygen, temperature, and yeast brought his *Manual* close to the most detailed oenological studies of his day. He also offered the first Bulgarian classification of wines: literally, 'wine for dinner and wine for after dinner'.

The presence of wine in Bulgarian National Revival literature is discreet, but distinctive. Wine is a constant subject in the dialogues between Hadji Gencho and Grandfather Liben in the classic novella *Bulgarians of Olden Times* by Lyuben Karavelov (1835–1879). The author uses it as a reference point in portraying the two characters. Their friendship is based on a shared love of wine, which they discuss fondly or quarrel fiercely about. Knowing and enjoying fine wine is an issue of honour and worldly wisdom for the two notables from Koprivshtitsa (a town that played a prominent role in the National Revival). The two men plunge into a lively discussion of wine in the very first scene of the book. 'Now tell me, Liben, which wine is better: Pastusha, Edren or Salavkievo?' Hadji Gencho asks on the porch of Grandfather Liben's house. 'Salavkievo wine is better,' the host replies and proceeds to explain that it 'tickles your throat and nips your tongue, while Pastusha sours only the tip of your tongue'. Disagreeing as usual, Hadji Gencho is of the contrary opinion. The two eventually start arguing about which wines are better. 'Old wine, old tobacco and old friends are always better than new ones,' Grandfather Liben concludes. Hadji Gencho notes that old wines are not good because they smell of yoghurt. He says this to keep up the conversation and to find an opportunity to praise Grandfather Liben's old wine, which one of his daughters-in-law would serve them later: 'I certainly don't want to argue with you and to have to prove that your wine isn't good, because I know very well that you understand wine and rack it when necessary and, besides, your vineyard is an old vineyard … better even than the vineyards in Cana of Galilee,' Hadji Gencho tells Grandfather Liben.

We can only speculate what the said wines were like. Pastusha is obviously Peroushtitsa wine (Pastusha is the name of a neighbourhood in the town of Peroushtitsa). As it improved by ageing, it must have been Mavrud. Edren wine is wine from Odrin (the Bulgarian name for Adrianople, now Edirne), whereas Salavkievo remains a mystery. To judge from Grandfather Liben's description, it must have been a distinctly fresh white, probably blended. Varietal wines were rare in that period.

The novella mentions one more wine. 'I've made sixteen casks this year, Hadji! I've also made a little cask of Krastavo village wine – you know, to have something to offer to poor folks,' says Grandfather Liben. According to another work by Lyuben Karavelov, *Notes on Bulgaria and the Bulgarians*, the village of Krastavo (now Krasnovo, near Plovdiv) was extremely poor. Obviously, its wine, probably Pamid, must have been quite humble too. The novella provides some interesting evidence about the daily consumption of wine. While arranging their children's marriage, Grandfather Liben offers his future in-law wine and explains:

This wine is fifteen years old, Hadji, and I didn't buy it; I made it from the grapes from my own Pastusha vineyard.

And do you have quite a bit of this old wine, Grandfather Liben?

About thirty buckets, Hadji.

This makes around 400 litres, and Hadji Gencho quickly starts calculating how long it will take to drink it up so that he can keep postponing the marriage until then: 'If one drinks two oka [oka = 1.3 litres] a day, in one month he is going to drink sixty oka; in two months – one hundred and twenty…' Obviously, two *oka*, or 2.6 litres, a day was considered more or less acceptable. The alcohol content of most wines in those days was not high, as later studies have found: it was 9–10%. That is why they oxidised and soured quickly, and that is also why Hadji Gencho says old wines smell of yoghurt. But Grandfather Liben's old Peroushtitsa wine was obviously different.

There are also references to wine in the works of Ivan Vazov (1850–1921), the father of Bulgarian literature. The cheap sour wine offered by one of the characters in his novella *Unloved and Unwanted* heightens passion in the eyes and conversations of the Bulgarian revolutionaries who fled to Romania before the liberation and dreamed of their country's independence. The wine in Vazov's novella *Old Chaps* is entirely different. 'They dropped by for a quick glass of Kisseler wine, which was the most famous wine because it was the wine favoured by teachers,' Vazov writes. It is under the influence of this particular wine that one of the characters later proclaims the lines that have become a classic quotation in Bulgaria: 'Arise, brave Bulgarians! Enough of slavery and tyranny! Brothers! The air trembles!' Such alcohol-induced, highly emotional but futile outbursts in the heady and heated discussions about revolt, uprising and conspiracy on the eve of the liberation must have inspired the classic Bulgarian poet Hristo Botev (1848–1876) to write his memorable line from the poem 'In the Pub': 'Hard the times are. Pass the wine jar!'*

Vines and wine figure prominently in the opening scene of Ivan Vazov's classic novel *Under the Yoke* (1894) – a chronicle of the trials of the Bulgarians under Ottoman rule – in which Chorbadji Marko and his family are having supper on a cool May evening. 'The master's table had been laid as usual, under the vine,' begins the second sentence of the novel. The servant girl pours wine into a deep porcelain dish, which Chorbadji Marko passes round to his children, saying benevolently: 'Drink, you rascals!' Wine here is not simply a graphic detail, but an omen of the coming stormy and bloody fermentation in which the entire Bulgarian people would be involved in the uprising against the Turks in April and May 1876 with the same passion and intensity with which Chorbadji Marko's children drink from the shared dish.

Page 88–89: **Rachenitsa** ***(Bulgarian folk dance), Ivan Mrkvička, 1896***

* *Translated by Peter Tempest*

The Wine of Independent Bulgaria

Bulgaria's liberation from Ottoman rule in 1878 found local vineyards in good condition. According to some statistics, in the late 1870s, vineyards occupied between 85,000 and 100,000 hectares. Soon after, however, disaster struck, as phylloxera reached Bulgaria and started to destroy the old plantations. The first to be hit in 1883 was the area of Vidin (northwestern Bulgaria), from where phylloxera gradually spread across the entire Danube plain. In the early twentieth century, it also affected the southern part of the country. The blight reached Melnik last, in 1912. By 1919, Bulgaria's vineyards had shrunk to 45,000 hectares, and it was not until 1938 that they recovered their pre-phylloxera acreage.

Drawing on the experience of Western European countries, the Bulgarian authorities took reasonably swift measures against the vine plague. They created several nursery gardens for vines grafted on to American rootstock. The prominent French expert Pierre Viala arrived in the country at the invitation of the Ministry of Agriculture and Trade in 1896. After touring all Bulgarian viticultural regions, he wrote a special report in which he suggested which American phylloxera-resistant rootstock was best suited to the different kinds of soil in the country. The report also recommended some other innovations of modern viticulture – for example, replacing vine-hooks by secateurs, and abandoning the custom of mixing grape varieties in small areas (a practice which, unfortunately, still continued for many years). Viala praised the Bulgarian varieties Mavrud, Pamid and Misket, recommending the first two – and especially Mavrud – as the main varieties for red wine production in southern Bulgaria. He thought that the most suitable variety for northern Bulgaria was Gamza, but

Bulgarian postcard of 1906

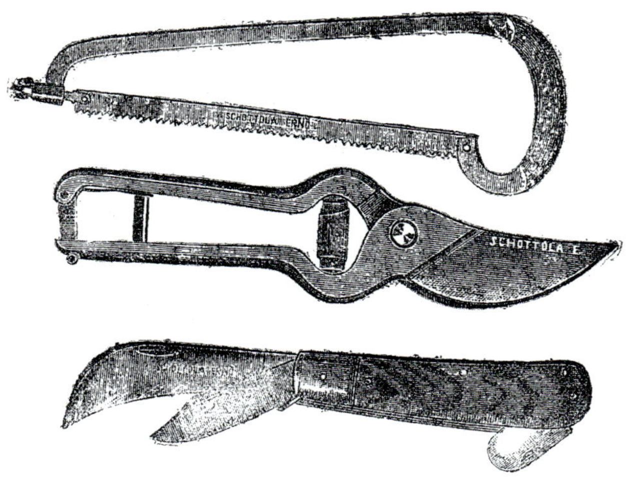

Grape harvest near Belovo, Bulgaria, 1929

Returning from the Grape Harvest, *Anton Mitov, 1893*

after some selection. The French expert believed that well-made Miskets could rival famous Hungarian and Rhine whites. In addition, he suggested introducing French varieties such as Gamay Noir, Syrah, Sémillon and Sauvignon Blanc in Bulgaria.

In 1902, on Prof. Viala's recommendation, Bulgaria's first vine and wine experimental station was established in Pleven; several decades later, it was transformed into a national institute, which is still in place. Notably, this was the fourth vine and wine experimental station in Europe. The first one was established in Italy in 1872, the second in France in 1874, and the third in Hungary in 1898. Although the French expert defined the natural factors in Bulgaria as particularly favourable for vine-growing, his opinion of the state of winemaking was not encouraging. 'Wine production is on the whole run quite badly and cellar installations are badly understood. Great improvements are required to ensure production of consistently good wines free from bad flavour, clear and durable.'

The state of Bulgarian winemaking and all its flaws are described in considerably greater detail in a 'Report to the Minister of Trade and Agriculture' by Stefan T. Gudev, assistant director at the ministry (1896). The report indicates that Bulgaria's vineyards were distributed among 366,000 owners, meaning an average of 0.266 hectares per vine-grower. (Another official document from the period notes that just 223 owners in the country had vineyards that exceeded 0.4 hectares.) Considering that each of those vine-growers made his own wine, it is apparent that consistent and high quality would have been the exception. 'When wine is made in small amounts one can never observe all conditions required for the proper fermentation and subsequent storage of wine,' Gudev writes. 'A small winemaker who makes wine only from his one or two, or let it be even ten decares [1 decare = 0.1 hectares] of vines would be reluctant and cannot afford to build a separate wine cellar, where he will not keep onions and garlic.' The other flaws noted include the mixing of green and ripe grapes, and the custom of leaving the marc in the wine to the very last, which was common in some regions (Vidin and Vratsa). Elsewhere, winemakers would leave the marc in the wine from 24 hours (Suhindol) to 40 days (southern Bulgaria). Where racking was more commonly practised (Sliven, Suhindol and Chirpan), the prices of wines were always slightly higher. The wine was racked by means of buckets and coppers. Only several people in Plovdiv and Sofia had introduced wine pumps. Although it is obvious that the country was not divided into winemaking regions according to specific types and quality of wine, we can deduce from the report that blacks prevailed in southern, reds in northern, and whites in eastern Bulgaria. In the early twentieth century, Bordeaux mixture and sprayers were gradually introduced in the country.

Considering the general state of winemaking, it seems almost incredible that some Bulgarian wines had already won prizes in Bordeaux, Budapest, Chicago, Antwerp and elsewhere. 'These are exceptions which we should never assume to be common and judge the quality of our wines on that basis alone,' Gudev argues. Curiously, the report indicates that urban owners of vineyards slightly outnumbered rural vineyard owners. After all, this means that quality was bound to improve sooner or later. That is the mission of urban culture.

The Interwar Upturn

Until the end of World War I, wine produced in Bulgaria was targeted exclusively at the domestic market. Viticulture remained very fragmented. Around 55% of Bulgaria's households grew vines and made wine. The majority of vineyards were small: 0.2–1 hectare. There were only a handful of larger winemakers, and typical and varietal wines were rare. Most wines were blended whites and reds, whilst batches with a distinct regional identity were produced only in some traditional winemaking centres such as Melnik, Assenovgrad, Suhindol, Sliven and Peroushtitsa.

The picture started to change gradually after the mid-1920s and in the 1930s, thanks to several

Part of the so-called Royal Collection of the wine cellar in Euxinograde, Bulgaria

dozen new vine and wine cooperatives that had their own wine cellars. The first cooperative was founded in Suhindol as early as 1909, and its example was soon followed in other parts of the country. Local producers drew on the experience of wine cooperatives from southern France. It is noteworthy that by that time Bulgarian oenologists trained in Austria, France, Italy and Germany were employed in wine production and readily shared their expertise by way of vine and wine newspapers and magazines.

Most cooperative wine cellars were of the classical type (with an underground section) and were built on the basis of standard designs from Western European countries. Their capacity ranged from 500 to 2,000 tonnes. The then Bulgarian Agricultural and Cooperative Bank contributed significantly to the development of wine production – in 1939 alone, it granted loans to twenty-four vine and wine cooperatives and already had eleven cellars of its own, plus another five leased out to cooperatives for long-term purchase. The majority used modern equipment, which they bought mainly from Austria, Italy and Germany. In 1940 Bulgaria had around sixty larger vine and wine cooperatives, which gradually started bringing the national wine industry closer to European standards of production and quality.

In the 1930s, the following main grape varieties were grown in Bulgaria's vineyards, according to the magazine *Vine Review*: Pamid (46%), Gamza (15%), Misket (6.3%), Cinsault (2.5%), Mavrud (0.5%) and Broad Vine of Melnik (1%); other varieties accounted for about 27% of the total area. The interest in high-quality European varieties such as Cabernet Sauvignon and Riesling also dates

from the 1930s, but those varieties were yet to be planted in Bulgaria.

In the interwar period, Bulgaria continued to produce wine as a standard commodity for the domestic market. The efforts of individual producers to trade with Europe achieved modest results. Exports peaked in 1927 and 1928, when a total of around nine million litres of bulk (non-bottled) wine was exported to Germany and Austria. This wine was used mainly in blends to improve local brands, and was not sold under the label of Bulgarian wine.

Autumn in the area of Melnik, Bulgaria

The Vine and Wine Press and the Temperance Movement in Bulgaria

The Bulgarian vine and wine press dates from 1896 and the *Vine Farming Newspaper*, launched in Pleven but closed the following year. The second specialised periodical, the magazine *Vine*, was launched in 1902. In the early twentieth century Bulgarian vine-growers and winemakers had several important reasons to unite and intensify media communication. Phylloxera had caused serious damage in northern Bulgaria and was spreading slowly to the south of the Balkan Mountains. During that same period, tonnes of counterfeit wines appeared on the market. These problems were discussed by the editors of and contributors to *Vine* and *Vine Newsletter* published by the vine-growers' trades union in Sliven and launched in 1904. Another two magazines appeared in 1911: *Vine-Grower* and *Nurseryman*. Besides phylloxera and counterfeits, the poor quality of imported rootstock was another main topic. Demands were made for concessions and incentives for Bulgarian nurseries. The two magazines offered all kinds of useful advice and tips on vine-growing and winemaking, as well as extensive international news. Among the other noteworthy specialised newspapers and magazines in the interwar period were *Vine, Wine and Pomicultural News*, *Winemaker's Newspaper*, *Vine Review*, *Winemaking*, *Liquor Seller*, *Liquor Seller's Defence* and *Suhindol Voice*.

The late 1920s saw the beginning of a particularly dynamic period in the history of this narrowly specialised press. After World War I, the temperance movement – organised in Masonic-like

г. I. София, 10 юлий 1929 г. Брой 4

ВИНО

УРЕЖДА РЕДАКЦИОНЕНЪ КОМИТЕТЪ
Редакция и администрация
София—ул. Алабинска 24
Телефонъ 4931
ИЗЛИЗА
ТРИ ПЪТИ ВЪ МЕСЕЦА

АБОНАМЕНТЪ
За България 100 лв.
За странство 150 лв.
ОБЯВЛЕНИЯ
3 лв. на квадрат. см.

Независимъ вестникъ за защита правата и интереситѣ на питиепродавцитѣ и лозаритѣ

lodges with names such as *Revival*, *Light* and *Forward* – became increasingly popular in Bulgaria. About a dozen temperance newspapers and magazines appeared, and the majority of them were supported by various Protestant churches. One of the few exceptions was the newspaper *Teetotal Railwayman*, which produced a single issue in 1934.

The most influential temperance periodical was the magazine *Fighting Alcoholism*, published from 1922 to 1941 in ten issues a year. It included a children's supplement called *Spirits Hater*, later renamed *Little Teetotaler*. The magazine offered mostly didactic articles in a moralising tone, with uniform headlines such as 'Alcohol and Tuberculosis', 'Alcohol and Sex', 'Alcohol and Children', 'Alcohol and Railways', 'Alcohol and the Liver', 'Alcohol and Influenza' and 'Aviators and Alcohol'. In them, wine was condemned as the number one enemy of humanity. One cannot help smiling at the zealous efforts of a Protestant pastor to prove that there was no evidence whatsoever that Christ and His disciples had actually drunk wine at the Last Supper and, even less that it had been fermented wine. That is why, the pastor argued, milk may also be used in the Holy Communion. The magazine's section on crime news reporting tirelessly in telegraphic style under the original subject heading 'From the Battlefield of Alcohol', is quite amusing too. The message is more than clear: almost every contact with wine and *rakiya* causes permanent disability or death.

The wine-loving Bulgarian public's attitude to the temperance societies was one of magnanimous tolerance. This lasted until 1929, when the hysterical enemies of alcohol were on the verge of a dangerous breakthrough in national politics. Several provisions that, if adopted, would have been disastrous for winemakers and tavern-keepers were included in the new National Health Bill. Article 172 prohibited policemen, and tram, cab and all other professional drivers (good clients, all of them), as well as all persons aged under 18, from entering taverns. Persons aged under 16 were prohibited from working in taverns and liquor stores. Article 175 of the bill was the severest of all: it provided for holding referendums on the closure of taverns in individual towns and villages. Those who were eligible to vote in the referendum were all persons aged over … 12! This fierce threat spurred winemakers and tavern-keepers to civic and political action. The first issue of *Pure Wine*, 'an independent newspaper defending the rights and interests of liquor sellers and vine-growers', came out on 1 June 1929. In the second issue, the newspaper was renamed simply *Wine*, probably in an effort to attract lovers of white wine, too, since most Bulgarians associate *ruyno*, or pure wine, with red wine. In a straightforward and outspoken keynote article, and in the best tradition of the Bulgarian political press, the newspaper warned in its very first issue: 'Wine producers and vine-growers, the danger is close. There is persistent talk in influential circles about introducing the Prohibition in Bulgaria too. Some MPs and public figures are already campaigning for this harmful idea. … Be on the alert and ready for battle!'

The keynote article defined the newspaper's mission as 'the fight against anti-alcohol organisations and their misinformation of the public'. Its other tasks included interpretation of fiscal laws and 'the fight against the efforts of the state to obstruct the proper development of winemaking and tavern-keeping'. *Wine* offered blisteringly critical articles of the temperance movement and referendums on the closure of taverns and on total prohibition, analyses of the domestic and international market, food recipes and practical tips for winemakers, advertisements and humorous stories. It told how the puritans in the USA 'arrested' Voltaire's novel *Candide* because of passages extolling wine, and how they intended to censor the Bible, especially the verse in the Psalms that referred to 'wine that maketh glad the heart of man'. Lengthy articles explained the essence of Prohibition in the USA as a manifestation of a hypocritical government policy owing to which many people had started drinking excessively while others had become millionaires. According to *Wine*, purely economic interests required keeping Prohibition in place, because lifting it would take away the livelihood of thousands of 'otherwise honest Americans' who were getting steadily richer from the sale of illicitly distilled whisky. The motto, 'Wine is to the old as milk is to the young', appeared on the front page of every issue in boldface. That was in response to the motto of the temperance press: 'If wine is food, then the devil is God.'

A pithy article on 'The Role of Taverns in the Fight for Liberation' in the maiden issue must have aroused patriotic fervour. Tracing the role of taverns in the life of Lyuben Karavelov, Hristo Botev, G. S. Rakovski, Hadji Dimitar and other national heroes, the author concluded emotionally: 'The tavern is a sacred place in our historical past, which we should revere because we owe our national and spiritual independence to it.'

At the end of July, *Wine* ceased publication after producing only six issues. The reason for the sudden end of this remarkable newspaper becomes obvious from an editorial in *Liquor Seller* (1 July 1929), meaningfully headlined 'A String of Successes'. The editor proudly summed up the results of the journalistic battles against the temperance movement: 'In the past few years, liquor sellers have scored several major successes. They have thwarted the adoption of those passages in the National Health Bill that threatened their existence, and have rallied in a steadfast ideological and militant organisation.' Naturally, once the dangerous provisions had been expunged from the bill, there was no point in continuing to publish *Wine*.

Bulgarian Wine Advertising in the Early Twentieth Century

If it is true that advertisements can reveal what a nation's ideals really are, as some experts claim, then wine advertising in Bulgaria in the early twentieth century does not reveal the Bulgarians as great connoisseurs of fine wine. This specific genre emerged at the turn of the century, when, because of phylloxera, the market was virtually flooded with counterfeits made from raisins, spirit, water, elderberry juice and so on. It was because of those counterfeits that 'pure' and 'natural' became key words in press advertisements. Other words and phrases that must have made wine more attractive for the drinking public were 'sound and cheap', 'old', 'matured', 'excellent' and, very rarely, 'fine'. Also noteworthy was the effort of producers and dealers to introduce a new advertising language. Their products were either 'most natural' or 'purely natural'. Apparently, the plain word 'natural' was considered insufficiently forceful in suggesting the complexity of the treatment that the advertised products had undergone.

Advertisements from the period give quite an accurate idea of the tastes and state of the market in the early twentieth century. They are detailed, verbose and, in a way, honest, but, at the same time, they manage to say almost nothing about the taste, variety, vintage and/or vinification technique of the advertised wine. Yet, today it is quite easy to deduce such details from the texts of advertisements in the period. A good example is an advertisement in the Sliven-based newspaper *Advertiser* (1919): 'TRAVELLER, DO GET OFF THE TRAIN, TRAVELLER! At Zimnitsa station, ten feet after Ruscho's shop, Old Nikola is expecting you and there you'll always find warmth, matured Balkan wine and extra-quality pilin [wormwood wine], assorted alcoholic drinks and excellent food to go with them...' The phrase 'Balkan wine' (which in this context means 'wine from the Balkan Mountains', and not from the Balkan peninsula), sounds rather suspect because vines do not grow high in the mountains. Here the advertiser must have had in mind something like 'manly' and 'heroic', which are qualities that Bulgarians commonly associate with the Balkan Mountains. This hardly means fine wine, but it must have scored a direct hit with Old Nikola's target group.

Wines were promoted in the press as white, red or black. Some advertisements also defined them as northern or southern. The names of individual wine centres were frequently mentioned as an indicator of quality. Readers were urged to buy Stanimaka, Pazardjik, Sliven, Suhindol, Pomorie or other local wines. Naturally, some regions were of greater interest than others, but there were no brands or appellations of origin in the modern sense of the word. The focus in advertisements was not on the product but on the person offering it. His name was usually highlighted graphically.

The frequent advertisements of 'essences, essential oils and dyes designed specially for alcoholic beverages' also give us grounds to question quality in that period. One advertisement explains ingenuously, 'Lis essences reproduce very accurately the smell of drinks promoted across the world, such as Greek cognac, fine champagne cognac and Scotch whisky.' This would have been somewhat more acceptable if it did not figure next to advertisements of 'most natural and pure white and red wines, mastika [aniseed-flavoured brandy], *rakiya*, liqueurs'.

The Wine of Communism

Winemaking became a state monopoly in the 1950s. Collectivisation led to enlargement of vineyards and to the gradual emergence of single-variety plantations, which is an essential condition for the introduction of standards and higher quality. Enlargement, however, made manual cultivation unprofitable, while the new tall-vine and wide-row training systems proved rather unsuitable for the traditional Bulgarian varieties. The introduction of machines necessitated moving vineyards from the hills to the plains, but this lowered the quality of wine.

In the 1960s and 1970s, Bulgaria's wine industry targeted almost exceptionally the huge and undiscriminating market of the Soviet Union and other Eastern bloc countries. Many of the large wine factories, with a processing capacity of up to 50,000 tonnes of grapes, were built at that time. The Georgian variety Rkatsiteli became quite popular, accounting for almost 40% of the white grape vineyards in the 1960s. At the same time, large areas were put under Cabernet Sauvignon and Merlot. Quality white grape varieties – Muscat Ottonel, Chardonnay, Sauvignon Blanc, Traminer Rosé – were also introduced, albeit on a smaller scale. By 1970, Bulgaria's vineyards covered around 200,000 hectares, of which 150,000 hectares were under wine grape varieties.

On the basis of the new varieties and following the introduction of modern vinification techniques, in the late 1970s and 1980s, the Bulgarian wine industry started to look for markets in the West and achieved some success in the UK, Germany, Japan, the USA and other countries. Around 90% of the wines were for export, still mainly for Russia and other Eastern bloc countries.

The practice of producing uniform blended wines, such as Voevodsko, Mecha Krav, Vecherny Zvon or Nashensko, which always had the same

Vinprom Shumen

Oriachovitza Wine Cellar

and not particularly impressive taste regardless of whether they came from Rousse, Stara Zagora or Varna, distanced the country for years from European standards, which are based on the uniqueness of every wine according to its origin and variety. That is why in Bulgaria it is impossible to produce statistics on the best vintages and crops in the past, comparable to those kept by all modern winemaking countries. In an effort to make a breakthrough in particular Western markets, in the late 1970s and 1980s Bulgaria started producing quality wines of controlled appellations of origin (Controliran) such as Merlot from Stambolovo, Melnik Wine from Harsovo, Gamza from Novo Selo or Chardonnay from Pomorie. The trend became possible thanks to the 1978 Wine Act, which introduced some French standards. Wines were classified into quality categories, with strictly regulated requirements for each category. The new Wine Act of 1999 complied with European regulations in winemaking. Its philosophy was based on the French concept of *terroir*, which is dominant in the so-called Old World.

Wine in Recent Times

At present, Bulgaria's wine vineyards cover approximately 120,000 hectares, and the trend is towards their further expanding. There are two reasons for the decimation of vineyards compared to 1970. After 1985, some of the vineyards were uprooted under the influence of Mikhail Gorbachev's crusade against drinking in Russia. Others were abandoned or uprooted in the early 1990s because of changes in land ownership after the fall of communism.

The varieties grown in the country are Cabernet Sauvignon (15%), Rkatsiteli (13%), Merlot (13%), Pamid (10%), Red Misket (8%), Dimiat (6.5%), Muscat Ottonel (6%), Chardonnay (3%), Gamza (1.6%), Riesling (1.3%), Ugni Blanc (1.3%), Broad Vine of Melnik (1%), Sauvignon Blanc and Traminer (sharing 1%); other varieties account for 20%. In the case of white grape varieties, the share of Chardonnay, Sauvignon Blanc and Traminer is growing at the expense of areas under

Domaine Boyar Blueridge – Sliven

Dimiat and Rkatsiteli. As regards black grape varieties, plantations of Cabernet, Merlot, Mavrud, Broad Vine of Melnik and Gamza are expected to increase, unlike those of Pamid. Some vine-growers are inclined to experiment with varieties new in Bulgaria but popular across the world, such as Pinot Noir, Syrah, Malbec, Zinfandel or Brunello.

In 1991 the state monopoly on winemaking was abolished, and in the following years all wine cellars were privatised. Bulgaria currently has more than eighty industrial wineries with a capacity between 100 and 80,000 tonnes. Bulgarian wine is sold in the UK, Germany, the Netherlands, the Scandinavian countries, the USA, Japan, Poland, Russia, and other countries. The UK accounts for the largest share of exports.

Bulgarian wine became known and attractive to Western Europe (mainly the UK) long before the fall of the Berlin Wall. In the 1980s, Bulgarian Cabernets and Merlots were very popular because they offered good value for money. As some British experts admit, 'Bulgaria' at that time became a synonym of a bottle of Cabernet or Merlot for £3. Sales peaked in 1995 and 1996, then started to decline sharply, dropping, in just a few years, to

Vineyards by the village of Karabunar near Plovdiv, Bulgaria

less than 50% of their 1996 levels. There were two main reasons for that. The first was a product of strong competition from the so-called New World wines, which had changed the structure of the international wine market for good. The other was a consequence of the privatisation of Bulgaria's largest wineries which sent shock waves throughout the industry; the post-1991 land reform also affected vineyards badly. As a result of land restitution, vine plantations were broken up into small land plots held by numerous owners, who had suddenly acquired the vineyards but had no idea what to do with them. Controlling grape quality became a significant problem for winemakers. During the period 1997–2000, shortages pushed grape prices above reasonable levels every autumn. Grapes were often picked before they had ripened, and no technological tricks could eliminate the green flavour of wine.

With a share of 2% of the world market, Bulgaria is currently among the top 15 wine-producing countries. Still, Bulgarian wines do not have a distinct identity and market niche. Generally, they are sold in the low-price categories and clients often abandon them when they find better value for money.

In the past few years, the wine industry has vacillated between the French concept of *terroir* and the promotion of wines with brand names that are not strictly connected with vine micro-regions. For example, if a red (Cabernet or Merlot) from a wine cellar in northern Bulgaria has a distinct fruity flavour of ripe grapes, and if it is full-bodied and concentrated, the grapes for that wine most likely came from southern Bulgaria. It must be admitted, however, that some of those new wines, in which the priority is the brand name, have actually proved better than the so-called quality wines produced in specified regions. It is easy to explain why – technological modernisation in wine cellars has outstripped significantly the development of vine-growing.

Vineyards by the village of Brestovitza near Plovdiv, Bulgaria

Purchasing grapes in Ivailovgrad

The processes under way in the industry remain quite dynamic. In the past few years, there has been a steady growth in investments in vine-growing. Bulgaria's leading wine producers and oenologists have realised that the demanding Western connoisseur may be attracted only by good-quality, albeit not large, batches. There are now a number of comparatively small cellars which are trying to make such wine – and some are succeeding. If they are grown on appropriate sites, with carefully controlled yields and have an appropriate marketing policy, Bulgarian grape varieties such as Mavrud and Melnik can make Bulgarian wine fashionable and bring it out of the purgatory of low shelves in Western supermarkets in the near future. It is noteworthy that in recent years Bulgaria's suitable soils and climate have started attracting foreign investors in wine production. If the natural resources are used adequately, the country may still have something to add to the image of grape varieties grown worldwide, such as Cabernet and Merlot. Wine is a domain of differences. Tastes, like fashions, change. And perhaps the day is not far off when a wine-drinking public that has had more than enough of French, Californian and Australian Cabernet, Merlot or Chardonnay may direct their interest to a somewhat different wine born in the land of Homer's Thracians.

Vinivel Ltd – Ivailovgrad

The Artificial Wine That Has Become Popular in France

When something went wrong and the vines did not yield fruit, people in France started making artificial wine for home consumption, and in copious amounts too! They prepare this wine as follows: Take a bucket three quarters full of boiling water and add 10 *zolotniks* [1 zolotnik = 1.3 grammes] of elder blossoms and 14 *zolotniks* of violet blossoms (if not available, use ground violet root), boil for several minutes, strain through a cloth and pour the liquid in a keg. Blend in 10 pounds of fine sugar, stirring with a paddle or stick. Add eight more buckets of water, three quarters of a bottle of fine wine vinegar, 15 *zolotniks* of fine hops and 4 *zolotniks* beer yeast: mix all this vigorously, cover it and leave it in the cellar for a few days. Finally, pour it in bottles and plug the bottles.

It is claimed that this cheap drink is quite nice and healthy.

Recipe from Petko R. Slaveykov's *Cookbook*,
Constantinople, 1870

Good Pilin and Bulgarian Champagne

Good pilin [wormwood wine] is made as follows: Layer black grapes and wormwood (a bitter and fragrant herb) in casks, then add overripe wine or curdled must and, plugging up the cask, leave it until spring. This is an excellent and delicious drink. Some wealthy Bulgarians will leave several casks full of wine outdoors, and when the casks freeze in winter, they will drill a hole in the bottom, drain off the wine, and pour it into glass bottles which they resinate and seal well, adding a little sugar and several drops of wine. The bottles are buried in straw in the cellars in winter, and in sand in summer. This is Bulgarian champagne, which is superior to the European one.

G. S. Rakovski, *Introduction*, 1859

From the Battlefield of Alcohol

Pernik: On 13 September the notoriously intemperate mechanic Ivanov, who is divorced from his wife, visited her in high spirits, wounded her and killed himself.

Sofia: On 17 September V. K. Koeva, aged 4, was left home alone, found a bottle of *rakiya* and started drinking. Death!

Tsarsko Selo, Chirpan: On 6 October Mito D. Mitov, aged 18, got drunk, quarrelled with his friend Koyu Irimov, aged 15, and killed him with a dagger. Short and straight, young friends!

Sofia: On 20 October Bozhura Manolova from the village of Zhedna, near Radomir, who lives near the station, was found unconscious in the Boris Public Gardens in the evening. In the hospital, the doctors found the following: she had drunk a lot of alcohol!

Sofia: On 11 August I. M. Itsovski, P. M. Andreev resident at 33 Vozhburn St, and M. P. Stamatov, 15 Kachanik St, got very drunk at Mino□s Steak pleasure haunt, on Tutrakan Blvd, and decided to kill the servant Doncho. They went out and starting firing revolvers. Doncho returned fire with a carbine and shot Itsovski.

Nadezhda, Sofia: On 14 July a fight broke out at a wedding between tipsy guests armed with knives and poles. B. Mitov was wounded in three places, M. Nikolov had his nose and upper lip cut off (he□s now ready for the circus!), V. Kirov (a policeman!) got 5 wounds and lost consciousness. After all, you can have only one perfect wedding in your life!

Fighting Alcoholism, No. VII–VIII, 1929

A Ripe Idea

Extremist dogmas of temperance, which dry up the creative potential of the people, kill individuality and usurp collective will, have long been a cause for serious alarm abroad. The indignant human conscience all over the world is rebelling against those sectarian utopias and waging a war against extremist ideas of temperance. It is only we who have remained passive onlookers, listlessly watching them perform their dastardly deeds; onlookers who are unwilling to take a stand and repel the attacks aiming to destroy the people's livelihood, to upset Bulgaria's agricultural and economic life.

We read and hear the same thing day after day: that we must not smoke or drink, or eat meat; in other words, that we must vegetate, stifle all emotions, all creative impulses, because they are supposedly bad for our physical and mental health...

Through newspapers and magazines, through sermons in towns and villages, this sectarianism is striving to penetrate all social strata, to change the pulse of our life... In some places it has achieved results that are good for them: they have used referendums to shut down taverns, open vegetarian eateries and temperance homes; they are living a secret life because they are in conflict with themselves: it is not so easy to resign oneself to physical and mental vegetation!

However, not only individuals and groups who are well aware of the total deception of extremist teetotallers, but also public circles are already considering the idea of waging a war against the extremist usurpers of human will and conscience.

Leading article, *Wine*, No. 2, 10 July 1929

The Dubious Holiness of Trifon Zarezan

Vines and wine have always been at the centre of the festival of Trifon Zarezan (literally, Trifon the Trimmer or Trifon the Cutter), and Bulgarians rarely consider the question of who, exactly, is the canonised saint whose feast day is 1 February, the day before the Presentation of Christ in the Temple. The truth is that St Tryphon has nothing to do with the Trifon who is venerated in Bulgaria as the patron saint of vine-growers and winemakers.

St Tryphon Martyr lived in Phrygia, an ancient district in Asia Minor, in the third century. The son of devout Christians, he dedicated his life to God. He had healing powers and succeeded in healing the daughter of Emperor Gordian (238–244) of a grave mental illness. But Gordian's successor, Decius (249–251), persecuted the Christians, and Tryphon was killed after he refused to renounce his faith. There is no mention of vines or wine in his hagiography.

The patron saint of vine-growers in Bulgarian folklore is obviously an entirely different person with a different biography and, more importantly, a different character. In popular belief, Trifon Zarezan is not a martyr but a man with a terrible hangover who injured himself badly because of his bad manners. According to a legend that is popular throughout Bulgaria, on the fortieth day after the Nativity (that is, on the day of the Presentation of Christ in the Temple) the Holy Virgin, bearing the Infant Christ, headed for the temple to pray for purification. On the way she met Trifon, who was going to his vineyard to trim the vines. She greeted him politely, but instead of greeting her back he laughed at her and told her that she was a 'maiden who had conceived before marriage'. The Holy Virgin went on her way (in some versions after cursing him, because in Bulgarian folklore even the Holy Virgin curses) and in a little while met Trifon's wife. She told the woman that she must go to the vineyard as fast as she could because her husband had cut his nose off. The Holy Virgin also told her to take strips of cloth, wool, eggs, lard, and other things which she would need for sticking and dressing. When Trifon's wife went to the vineyard she saw that there was nothing wrong with her husband. She told him about her encounter with the Holy Virgin, and Trifon retorted angrily: 'I'm not drunk ('mad', in some versions), am I, to cut my nose off!' And, wielding the knife, he went on: 'I don't cut this way but that!' And at that instance he really did cut his nose off. By and large, this is the popular perception of Trifon. He is known as the Trimmer or Cutter, and in some places as the Snub-Nosed, precisely because he cut off his nose. The legend ends here. But digging into its deep structural and semantic layers, ethnologists have peeled off the Christian garb of the characters, only to find the mythical figures of Thracian antiquity grinning wickedly back at them. With his rudeness to the Holy Virgin, Trifon is reminiscent of a character of ancient Greek mythology, who likewise contrived his own undoing: Lycurgus, king of the Edones in Thrace. Lycurgus banned his subjects from worshipping the god of wine and revelry, Dionysus, persecuted his priestesses and ordered all vines to be uprooted. The gods punished him by driving him mad and blinding him. In a fit of rage, he once tried to cut off a vine but instead cut off his legs or, according to some versions, killed his son. The legend of Trifon Zarezan partly reinterprets the ancient myth with different characters. Both tell of the same crime (Lycurgus offended the god of wine, and Trifon insulted the Holy Virgin) and of virtually the same punishment: Lycurgus cut off his legs, while Trifon got away with a cut-off nose, which his loving wife stuck back in place, using the wool, lard, eggs and other things that the Holy Virgin had advised her to bring along.

St Trifon Zarezan, ***Bulgarian icon, nineteenth century. By tradition, Bulgarian icon painters represent him with a slightly deformed nose***

This dual nature of St Tryphon or Trifon is also reflected in Bulgarian icons. Some nineteenth-century icon painters represent the canonised saint holding a vine-hook and sometimes with a slightly deformed nose. The real reason that Christian saints appear in stories that can be traced back to pagan antiquity is wine. In the Bulgarian festival of wine, Trifon Zarezan, it is not difficult to discover echoes of the loud and boisterous Dionysian mysteries that were once celebrated in Bulgaria on the eve of spring.

Traditional Bulgarian Wine Grape Varieties

Dimiat: a very old, native white grape variety. It is grown throughout the country, and especially around Burgas and Varna. A late-ripening variety, Dimiat ripens in the first half of October in the eastern (Black Sea) region and in late September in southern Bulgaria. It produces fine table whites, straw yellow with a light greenish tinge in colour,

with a delicate, fresh and slightly fruity, usually peachy, bouquet, and a harmonious taste. This variety is also used in distillates for Bulgarian wine brandy.

Red Misket: grown on Bulgarian territory since ancient times, mainly in the Rose Valley and the areas of Plovdiv, Burgas, Haskovo and Varna. This variety currently accounts for around 8% of Bulgaria's wine vineyards. It ripens in late Sep-

tember and early October. The grape makes quality dry whites, with an attractive straw yellow colour, harmonious taste and specific varietal bouquet with hints of apple, honey and herbs. Owing to its low acidity, Red Misket is commonly blended with white grape varieties.

Pamid: a very old, native black grape variety grown even by the ancient Thracians. This used to be the most widely-cultivated variety in southern Bulgaria, and the second most planted one (after Gamza) in northern Bulgaria. Around 11% of Bulgaria's wine vineyards are currently under Pamid. It is comparatively resistant to cold and drought, and not very demanding as regards soil. The grapes are best when grown on hilly terrain with light, warm and porous soils. This variety produces relatively simple light, dry table reds for mass consumption, light red or rosy in colour. Their low acidity and concentration makes them unsuitable for ageing.

Gamza: a native variety grown since ancient times. Elsewhere in Eastern Europe it is known as Kadarka. Gamza used to be the main wine grape

variety in northern Bulgaria, but currently occupies less than 2% of the country's wine vineyards. It ripens in late September or early October. Gamza wines are ruby red, with a distinct varietal bouquet with raspberry undertones and a slightly resinous finish. They have comparatively high acidity and low tannin content. When aged for two or three years, they develop a mellow and pleasantly fresh, harmonious taste.

Mavrud: a high-quality, native black grape variety grown since ancient times. Today it is cultivated mainly around Plovdiv and Assenovgrad, occupying less than 1% of the country's vineyards. A warm-loving and demanding variety,

Mavrud grows best on deep, alluvial soils with good water-retention properties, in warm areas with a cumulative temperature of over 4,000 degrees Celsius during the growth period, where temperatures in winter do not fall below minus 16 degrees. Depending on the year, the grapes have a sugar content of 18–22% at 6.5 to 10 gramme/litre acidity. They are very rich in extract and in colour substances. Mavrud wines are dark red in colour with a garnet tint, full-bodied, with red and black forest fruit on the nose. They are very suitable for ageing. When aged in oak barrels, they develop a chocolaty bouquet with notes of black pepper and cinnamon.

Broad Vine of Melnik (Shiroka Melnishka Loza): a high-quality black grape variety grown in a micro-region around the town of Melnik and the villages of Harsovo, Marikostinovo, Krapatovo, Vinogradi and others. Late-ripening and warm-loving, this variety develops its best qualities only in the southwesternmost part of Bulgaria, where the cumulative temperature during the growth period exceeds 4,000 degrees Celsius and where there are distinct Mediterranean climatic influences. The grape produces deep reds that are highly concentrated. The younger wines have a distinct flavour of cherries and black forest fruit. Barrel ageing enhances the bouquet adding black pepper, tobacco, leather and other characters. The wines are suitable for ageing. The variety Early Vine of Melnik (Ranna Melnisha Loza, Melnik 55), (Uniqato wine), is a clone of Broad Vine of Melnik. It was produced in 1955 from Broad Vine of Melnik and mixed pollen of Durif, Jurançon and Valdige. In the Melnik region it ripens around 20 to 25 September, or two weeks earlier than Broad Vine of Melnik.

Rubin: a comparatively new Bulgarian wine grape variety. It was produced in Pleven in the 1950s by crossing Syrah and Nebbiolo. This variety is grown in small areas around Plovdiv and Svishtov. It makes excellent reds, full-bodied and firm, with red fruit and flowers on the nose. Blended with Cabernet Sauvignon or Merlot, it produces excellent wines. Rubin is suitable for ageing. It is definitely a variety with a future.

Otel: this variety is not grown commercially but is quite common in private vineyards in northwestern Bulgaria. Otel is a native American variety (*Vitis labrusca*). It is very productive and, therefore, favoured by small vine-growers. Otel appeared in Bulgaria at the turn of the twentieth century as a result of phylloxera. Obviously in an effort to economise, many vine-growers in the period planted the rootstock directly, without grafting the cultivated vine (*Vitis vinifera*). Otel produces heavy, deeply coloured and tart wines with unpleasant and extremely pronounced flavours. Foxy flavour is a common flaw. Planting of Otel for wine production is prohibited.

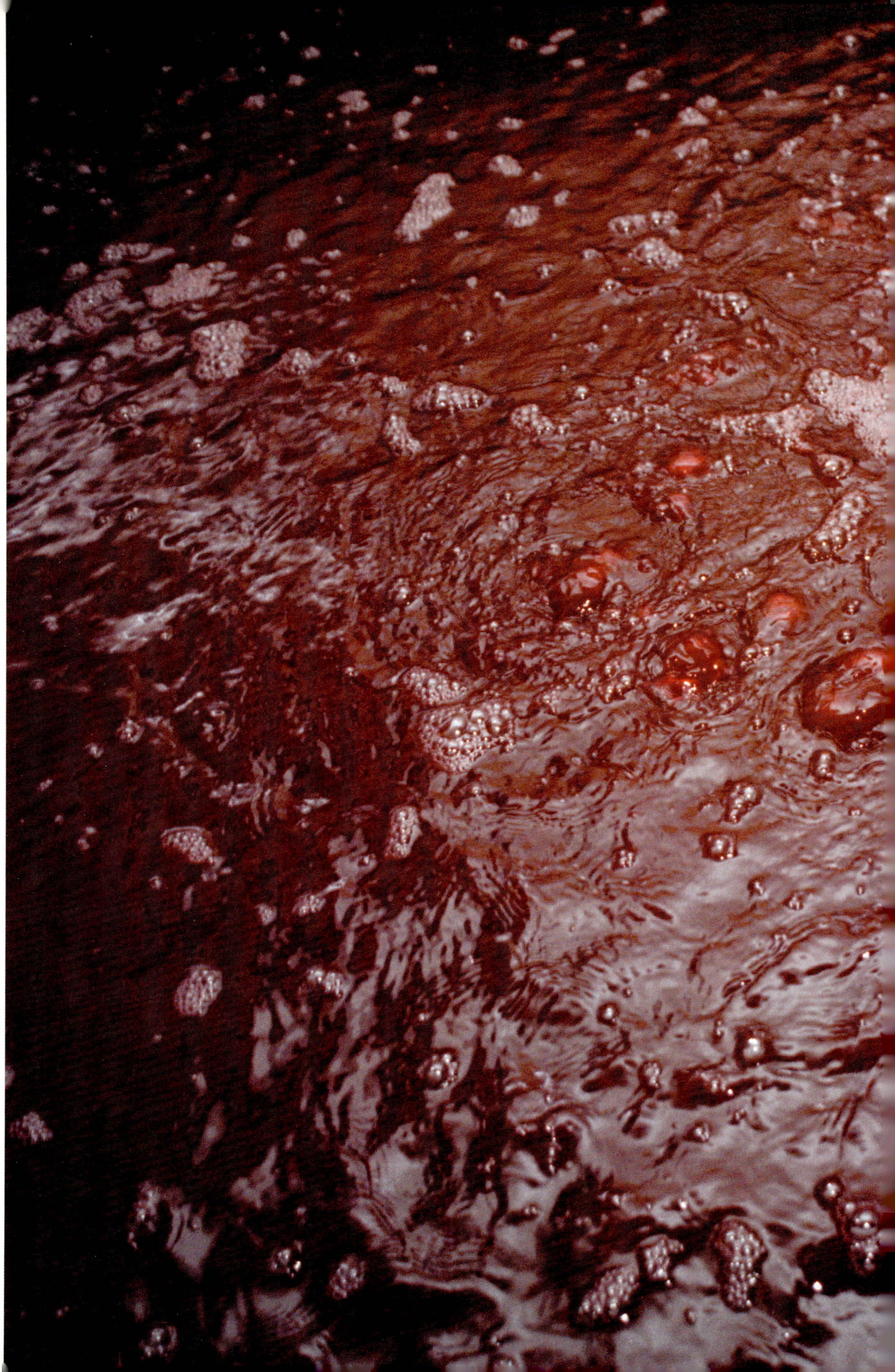

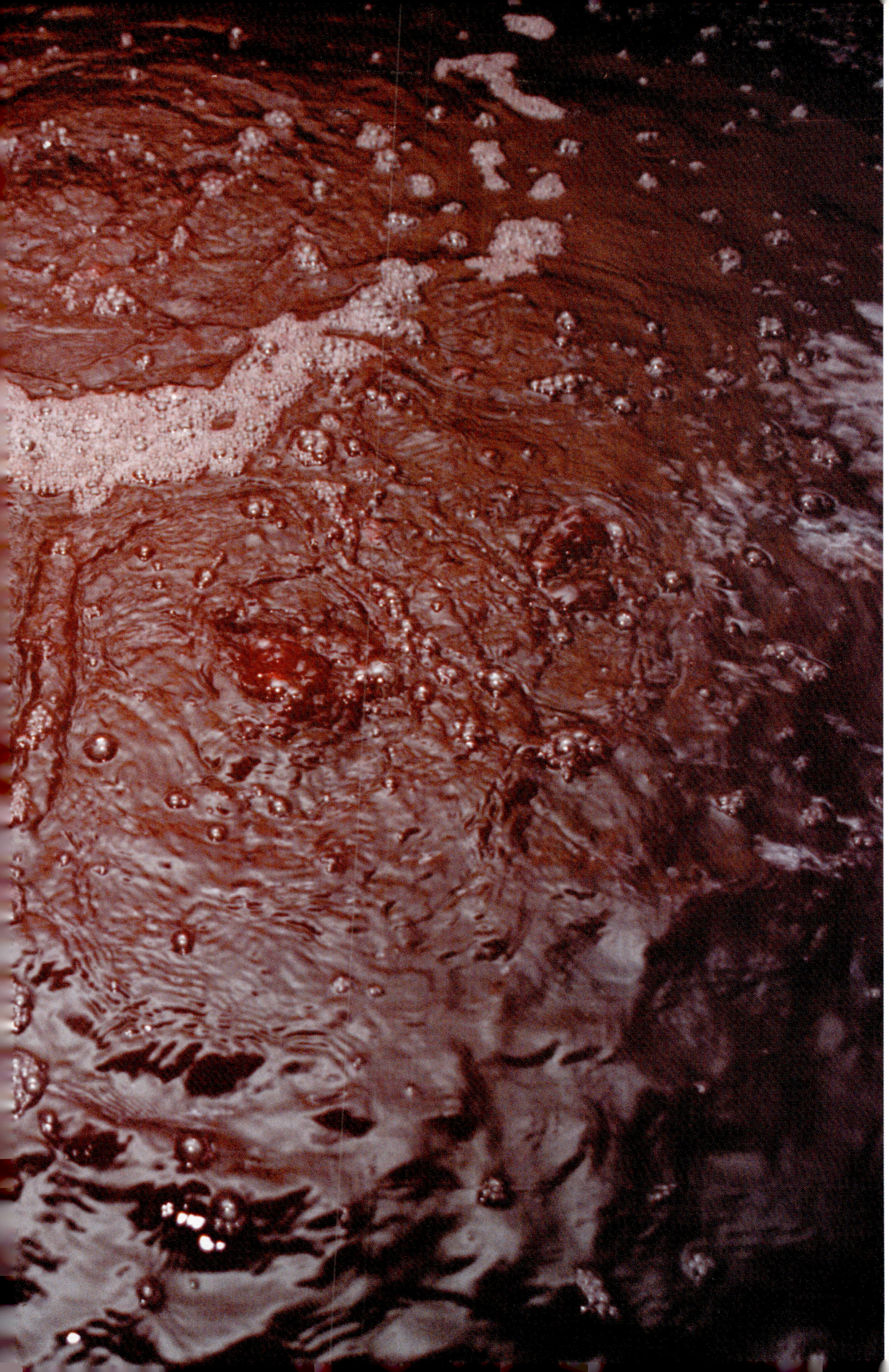

International Wine Grape Varieties Grown in Bulgaria

White Grape Varieties

Chardonnay: a classic French variety, also known as Pinot Blanc and Pinot Chardonnay. It is currently considered the greatest dry white wine grape in the world and is grown in virtually every commercial wine-making area. This is one of the three major grape types used in the production of Champagne. Grown on poorer limestone and rocky soils (as are most soils in the region of Chablis), it makes wonderful and very delicate dry wines.

Some Chardonnays from Australia, California and France have complex and attractive undertones of hazelnuts, bitter almonds, acacia, and toasted bread. These flavours, however, depend both on the variety and on the vinification technique. The bouquet most often has hints of apple, melon, pineapple and citrus (grapefruit and lemon). In Bulgaria, this variety produces good wines in the regions of Preslav, Razgrad, Pomorie and Sungurlare.

Sauvignon Blanc: a French variety cultivated in most wine countries in the world. It grows best on poor rocky and limestone soils. Sauvignon Blanc produces very good dry wines with a characteristic pleasant freshness when young. They usually have a hint of freshly cut grass in the bouquet, especially when the grapes come from cool-

er regions. A warmer climate makes the wines distinctly fruity, sometimes musky. This is the chief grape variety in many of the wines from Sauternes, Graves and Entre-Deux-Mers in France. It makes remarkable wines in New Zealand, where it is known as Blanc Fumé. In Bulgaria, it is grown mainly in the eastern (Black Sea) region.

Gewürztraminer: a classic German variety. In Bulgaria it is known as Traminer Rosé or simply Traminer. This variety is grown mainly in Alsace, Germany and Austria. It produces very opulent wines, usually with flowery bouquets dominated by roses. When the grapes are fully ripe, the flowery bouquets may develop into fruity ones, such as peach and apricot. In Bulgaria, Gewürztramin-

er was introduced in the 1970s, in small areas in the region of Shumen and Preslav. In recent years interest in this variety has been growing in other regions of the country, too.

Riesling: one of the oldest European varieties, originally from the region of the Rhine and Moselle (Germany). Numerous local clones, selections and hybrids of the Riesling are grown in most Europe-

an countries, as well as California, Australia, South Africa and elsewhere. The grape produces fine dry, but also medium dry and sweet wines. They are grassy, herby and slightly petrolly, and the medium dry and sweet wines have citrus-fruity characters (grapefruit, orange). In Bulgaria this variety is grown mainly in the eastern (Black Sea) region.

Rkatsiteli: a Georgian variety introduced in Bulgaria in the 1960s. In its country of origin it produces good sweet wines, but in Bulgaria its qualities are unimpressive. It is also known as Rikat. The grape has a weak bouquet. It makes wines that are very ordinary and usually have high acidity, and they are therefore commonly used in blends or distillates.

Muscat: a family name for numerous related varieties, sub-varieties, and localised clones of the same variety grown around the world. The wines that are produced range from dry to sweet. All have a distinctive candy-like character and a musky

bouquet reminiscent of ground coriander. Many have a hint of geranium on the nose. In Bulgaria the grape is known as Muscat Ottonel, Tamianka, and several other local varieties and sub-varieties.

Ugni Blanc: a very productive French variety grown in many wine-producing countries. It makes fresh and light wines with a weak, mainly floral, bouquet. In France it is the main variety in the production of cognac. In Italy this variety is known as

Trebbiano. In Bulgaria, Ugni Blanc is grown in the eastern (Black Sea) region, and is used mainly in distillates for wine brandy. Blended with Muscat, it makes pleasant, fresh wines.

Aligoté: a French variety grown mainly in Burgundy. It is also known as Giboudot. The grape produces slightly tart, full-bodied, but unexceptional wines that oxidise easily. In Bulgaria it is grown on limited areas, mainly in Lyaskovetz as well as other regions.

Black Grape Varieties

Cabernet Sauvignon: currently the best known and most widely-cultivated black grape variety. It is grown virtually worldwide; according to some data, it occupies around 10% of the

world's wine vineyards. It is vitally important to Bordeaux wines. The grape produces concentrated wines that are rich in tannin and colour, many of them being suitable for ageing. They have generous and complex bouquets that can vary greatly depending on the climate and soil. Young wines from warm years usually have red and black fruit (raspberry, cherry and blackcurrant) on the nose. The wines might develop green pepper, ginger and tobacco (cigars) characters. They do very well in contact with oak; when barrel-aged, they develop an excellent bouquet and round taste. In addition to the standard vanilla note, oaked wines can acquire hints of cinnamon and other spices, toasted bread and chocolate. In Bulgaria, Cabernet Sauvignon is grown all over the country but makes the best wines in the area around Svishtov and in the southern region.

Merlot: a French variety that rivals Cabernet Sauvignon in popularity and prestige. In the past it was also known as Vitraille. Merlot is grown in all winemaking countries. Young Merlots have softer tannins and are rounder than Cabernets;

therefore, the two varieties blend excellently. The wines usually have red fruit (ripe cherry and plum) on the nose; when barrel-aged, they develop a rich, lusciously fruity and velvety flavour that is complemented by oak. Some older wines from this variety have a characteristic bouquet of truffles. In Bulgaria, Merlot is grown all over the country, but mainly in the southern part, and it makes the best wines around Haskovo and Lyubimec.

Pinot Noir: a French variety grown mainly in Burgundy and Champagne (one of the classic varieties of the sparkling wines), but also in other wine-producing countries. In Germany it is also known as Schwartz Klevner. Under ideal climatic conditions, Pinot Noir can produce velvet-smooth

wines with exceptional finesse and bouquet, and a slightly brickish hue in colour. Cherries and raspberries are characteristic of the varietal flavour. Pinot Noir wines develop very well in contact with oak. In Bulgaria this variety is cultivated on very small areas, still on an experimental basis.

Bulgarian Oak Barrels

Cooperage was a very important trade in the past, and it was practised in all parts of Bulgaria. Wooden containers were used not only in wine production but also in other sectors of food-processing, as well as in everyday life. Today the largest producer of wine barrels in Bulgaria is the village of Vrachesh, 2 km from Blagoevgrad and 50 km from Sofia. Until 1990, the village had a large barrel-making factory that employed several hundred workers. Today the business is distributed among 30-odd family workshops, most of which make from 100 to 500 barrels a year. The main product is the standard 225-litre *barrique*, but containers of other sizes (from 10 to 1,000 litres) can be made to order too. There are also some barrel-

Wine cellar at Vinex Slavyantzi

Barrel-making workshop in the village of Vrachesh near Botevgrad, Bulgaria

making enterprises elsewhere in the country. Coopers use oak from Mt Strandja and some northern parts of the Balkan Mountains, mainly of the *Quercus robur* and, especially, of the *Quercus sessiliflora* species. The oak is split and seasoned outdoors for 18 to 24 months, and the barrels are toasted with oak blocks.

Bulgarian oak is tight-grained, with a fine texture and soft, deep tannins. Its chemical composition is close to that of French oak and, more specifically, oak of Limousin, in which some of the world's finest wines are aged. The coopers of Vrachesh will usually argue passionately that their barrels are better than the French and American ones, but experienced winemakers know that this is not always true. Their prices, however, are significantly lower than those of some French or American barrels.

Until recently, Bulgarian wineries used two types of barrels: barrels for storage and barrels for transportation of wine. Barrels for storage usually have a capacity of around 8 tonnes, but may vary in size. Some old cellars still store wine in barrels of 2–3, or 15–20 tonnes. Modern cellars tend to replace them with stainless steel vats, which are more hygienic and easier to maintain.

Following world wine fashion, Bulgarian winemakers use not only Vrachesh but also French and Californian barrels, because each oak adds a different flavour to the wine. Oak chips are also used occasionally in Bulgaria.

How to Read Bulgarian Wine Labels

The standards of what a label must say about the particular wine are more or less unified throughout the world, but every country or market has some specific requirements and signs. All wine labels give certain *obligatory* information; printing other information is *permitted* but likewise regulated in order to prevent misleading consumers.

In Bulgaria, the following information on wine labels is obligatory: product (wine), country of origin, producer's name and address, licence number, volume of the bottle, alcoholic content, name of importer (if the wine is imported), a mark identifying the lot (bar code), and, for sparkling wines, type (dry, brut). Permitted details include the colour, brand name, wine category, grape variety, style, vintage, geographical origin, production technique, ageing, and other information.

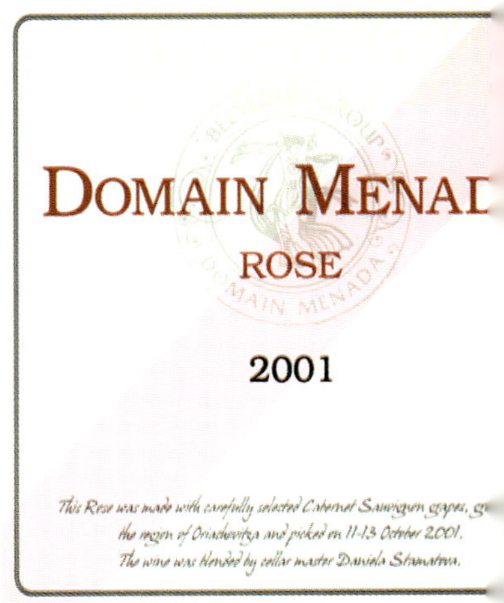

There are two categories of wine (according to the 1999 Wine and Spirit Drinks Act): *table wines*, and *quality wines produced in specified regions*. Quality wines produced in specified regions may be of guaranteed and controlled appellation of origin (GADO) or only of guaranteed appellation of origin (GAO). The corresponding designations of quality wines produced before the year 2000 are respectively wines of controlled appellation of origin (known as Controliran, CAO or AOC) and of declared geographical origin (DGO).

The grape variety may be indicated on the label only if at least 85% of the wine has been produced

from it. The vintage may be indicated only if 100% of the grapes are from the respective year. Information about the style and type of wine, blended varieties and production technique may be printed on the counter-label, which can also carry other details for which no space is available on the front label.

The most popular Bulgarian wines are not necessarily those of guaranteed and controlled appellation of origin. Some of the best Bulgarian wines (such as ReDark, No Man's Land, Uniqato, Maxima, Tcherga or Santa Sarah) are marketed as brand names without indicating the wine category on the label.

Bulgarian wines may not be designated as 'chateau'. This designation is subject to complicated legal regulation and may be used only for French *Appelation d'origine contrôlée* (AOC) wines that originate from genuine *chateau* estates. Still, it is used for some wines destined for markets that are not subject to EU wine law.

Page 118–119: Vineyards near Preslav, Bulgaria

chapter 4

Bulgarian Winemaking Regions, Cellars and Wines

Bulgaria's climate, landscape, and soils are excellent for vine-growing and winemaking. The country is on the boundary between the temperate continental and Mediterranean climatic belts. Bulgaria's numerous mountain ranges obstruct Aegean and Adriatic climatic influences, while the mainly western winds limit the Black Sea influence to a comparatively small part of the country. That is why the climate in Bulgaria is slightly cooler than that in central Italy or southern France, which are at the same latitude. According to the different soils and climatic conditions, the country is divided into several vine-growing and winemaking regions, each with its particular grape varieties and wines.

Bulgaria currently has more than 100 industrial wineries which produce bottled and bulk (non-bottled) wines that vary in quantity and quality. More than ten years since the start of privatisation the developments in the wine industry have remained very dynamic and as a result some of the information in any reference book on the subject will inevitably become outdated relatively quickly. This book presents only producers of bottled wines marketed under own brand names.

Northern Region (Danubian Plain)

The Northern Region spans the area between the Danube to the north and the Balkan Mountains to the south, including the micro-regions around Rousse (sometimes spelled 'Russe' or 'Ruse'), Byala and Gorna Oryahovitsa to the east. The cumulative temperature during the growth period varies between 3,500 and 3,980 degrees Celsius. Vine growth lasts from 180 to 213 days, starting between 5 and 15 April and ending between 15 and 25 October. The mean temperature in the hottest month (July) is 21–24 degrees Celsius. In winter the temperature may drop to 18 degrees below zero, putting vines in danger of freezing. The mean annual rainfall is 550–600 mm, and the rainfall is 90–100 mm in September and October. There are several dozen vine-growing micro-regions. The conditions are relatively favourable for black grape varieties: Cabernet Sauvignon and Merlot, as well as indigenous varieties such as Gamza and Pamid. Some white grape varieties – such as Chardonnay, Sauvignon Blanc, Aligoté, and Riesling – also make fine wines. The main wineries in the region are in Rousse, Svishtov, Pleven, Suhindol, Lyaskovets, and Vidin.

Bouquet Telish

Wine Cellar:
5990 s. Telish, obl. Plevenska, Bulgaria
tel: (+359 6575) 23 22
Trade Office:
1421 Sofia, ul. Lozenets No. 22, Bulgaria
tel: (+359 2) 963 1773
e-mail: telish@techno-link.com

The wine cellar in the village of Telish was built in 1967 as a subsidiary of Vinprom Pleven (the local branch of Vinprom, the state-owned company that held a monopoly of the wine industry in communist Bulgaria). Prior to privatisation in 1996, it was of local importance only. In recent years it has been significantly remodelled, extended and modernised. Its capacity approximates 4,000 tonnes. Bouquet Telish purchases from 1,500 to 2,500 tonnes of grapes (depending on the quality of the crop) mainly from two regions: the village of Varbitsa near Pleven and the village of Kolarovo near Harmanli.

The vineyards in Varbitsa occupy around 110 hectares and are under Cabernet Sauvignon only. The land is flat, about 240 m above sea level. Vine growth starts on 7 April and ends on 20 October. The cumulative temperature exceeds 3,800 degrees Celsius, and the mean annual rainfall is around 600 mm (370 mm during the growth period). The mean temperature in the hottest month (July) is 23 degrees Celsius. The soils are leached, moderately to highly weathered, airy, with a humus content of 3–4.5% and good heat-retention properties – in other words, they are very suitable for red wine varieties. The average yield is around 5,000 kg per hectare, with a sugar content of 22–23%.

The vineyards in Kolarovo occupy around 500 hectares, mostly under Merlot as well as some Cabernet Sauvignon and Pamid. The region lies around 150 m above sea level. The cumulative temperature during the growth period approximates 4,000 degrees Celsius, and the mean temperature in July is 23–24 degrees. The mean annual rainfall is 562 mm (350 mm during the growth period). The autumn is warm and dry, which is particularly important for the ripening of grapes. Most of the soils are cinnamonic forest, typical and leached, moderately to highly weathered, medium-heavy to heavy sandy clay, and relatively rich in humus.

The Bouquet Telish Wine Cellar specialises in the production of quality reds from Cabernet Sauvignon and Merlot grapes. It also offers more ordinary blended wines from various other grape varieties: Storgozia, Bouquet, Pamid, and others. Some wines are also available in bag-in-box packaging, making them very popular with small restaurants and pizzerias. In the last three years Telish Merlots and Cabernets have attracted the interest of connoisseurs with their rich and excellently balanced fruity taste achieved without contact with oak.

***Telish* Merlot 2001**: an impressive wine, lovely purple in colour, with a distinct varietal bouquet of ripe grapes with hints of raspberry, cherry and herbs, and a long and lasting aftertaste; gold medal at the international Concours Mondial du Vin in Brussels in June 2002, and silver medal at the International Wine and Spirit Competition in London in May 2002.

***Telish* Merlot 2002**: dark ruby red; intensely fruity nose with cherries, forest fruit and spice; well-balanced, fruity palate.

***Telish* Cabernet Sauvignon 2003**: dark red; very good structure, full-bodied; ripe and fruity bouquet with hints of raspberries, blackcurrant and forest fruit.

***Telish* Cabernet Sauvignon 2002**: dark ruby red; distinct varietal bouquet; well-structured taste with pleasant notes of cherries, forest fruit and spice.

Gamza 1922 Pleven

5800 Pleven, ul. Vit No. 7, Bulgaria
tel: (+359 64) 20 047, 31 588;
fax: (+359 64) 49 415

This winery was established in the early 1950s on the basis of earlier local vine and wine cooperatives. It was one of Bulgaria's leading wineries in the recent past. Some of its best wines (**Cabernet Sauvignon Selection Wine 1997** and **Lozitza Cabernet Sauvignon 1996**) are now marketed under the Avelis brand name.

Lozitza **Cabernet Sauvignon 1996**: deep ruby red showing some development on the rim; attractive nose with red fruit and smoke; mellow and pleasant palate.

Cabernet Sauvignon *Selection Wine* 1997: deep garnet in colour; attractive bouquet of red and black fruit; full-bodied taste with a good length and a slightly tart finish.

Lovico Suhindol

5240 Suhindol, ul. Rossitsa No. 156, Bulgaria
tel: (+359 6136) 35 140;
fax: (+359 6136) 30 20
e-mail: lovico@lovico.com

In Bulgaria, the name Suhindol has always been associated with vines and wine. This is where the country's first important vine-growing and winemaking cooperative, with its own wine cellar built and equipped according to European standards, was established in 1909.

The local Gamza cooperative was nationalised in 1949. Over the next decades, the cellar was repeatedly extended and modernised. Some Suhindol reds (mainly Cabernets and, to a lesser extent, Gamzas and Merlots) established Bulgaria's reputation as a wine country in the western markets in the 1980s. In 1991 the cooperative was restored under the name of Gamza Suhindol Vine and Wine Cooperative, and after a turbulent decade of successes and failures, it was finally acquired by the Varna-based TIM holding company in 2002. Two wines that can still be found on the market, Cabernet Sauvignon Estate Selection 1994 and Cabernet Sauvignon Special Selection 1996, are a reminder of Gamza Suhindol's best years. The winery's capacity is around 25,000 tonnes. The vineyards in the region occupy roughly 1,500 hectares, mainly around Suhindol and the villages of Byala Reka, Dimcha, Varbovka, Kramolin, and Koevtsi. The winery has a state-of-the-art wine

research and control laboratory in the town of Pavlikeni. It produces a wide range of whites and reds from Cabernet Sauvignon, Merlot, Muscat Ottonel, Chardonnay, Pamid, Dimiat, Riesling, and other grapes.

***Gamza Suhindol* 1999**: deep ruby red; pleasant cherry bouquet; typical varietal fresh taste with a touch of spice on the finish.

Lyaskovets Winery

5140 Lyaskovets,
Bulgaria
tel: (+359 619) 22 022;
fax: (+359 619) 24 846
e-mail: vinarna@gelesoft.com
www.winery.lyaskovec.com

This winery is the successor to the Pchela Cooperative, which was founded in 1924 and built a cooperative wine cellar in 1934. The winery itself was built in the 1960s and has subsidiary cellars in Ressen, Strazhitsa and Polski Trambesh. Their total capacity is around 30,000 tonnes. In the past the winery was best known for its natural sparkling wines as well as for the local Aligoté of controlled appellation of origin (Controliran). This is where the legendary Bulgarian sparkling wine Iskra was created at the end of the 1950s. Another two natural sparkling wines produced in Lyaskovets (sometimes spelled 'Lyaskovec' or 'Lyaskovetz') later became quite popular too: Severna Korona and Favourite.

The vineyards in the region (around 700 hectares) are generally on sandy clay, grey forest soils, at an altitude of 192–256 m above sea level. The cumulative temperature during the growth period is approximately 3,800 degrees Celsius. The mean annual rainfall is around 600 mm (350 mm during the growth period). The conditions here are more favourable for white wines. The grape varieties cultivated in the region are Chardonnay, Aligoté, Rkatsiteli, Dimiat, Pamid, Gamza, Cabernet, and Merlot. The Lyaskovets Winery produces a wide range of white and red dry, medium dry, and sparkling wines. It has wine tourism facilities.

Magura Winery

Wine Cellar:
3938 s. Rabisha, Belogradchishko, Bulgaria
tel: (+359 9329) 230; fax: (+359 9329) 312
Trade Office:
1407 Sofia, ul. Korab Planina No. 27, Bulgaria
tel: (+359 2) 868 1400, 868 6161
e-mail: ita_hold@spnet.net
www.magurawine.com

In its soils and climatic conditions, the region around Rabisha Hill (where this winery is located) is similar to that of Champagne in France, while the nearby Magura Cave provides excellent conditions for production of natural sparkling wines by the classical bottling method – a permanent temperature of 12 degrees Celsius and appropriate humidity. This is the only place in Bulgaria where such wines are produced by that method.

The cellar was built and linked by a tunnel to the wine section of the Magura Cave in 1968. In recent years, the Magura Winery has been doing quite well on the market. It is best known for its natural sparkling wines from Rkatsiteli, Chardonnay, and Aligoté grapes. The most prestigious among them are those in the Golden Classics range. The winery also produces good Gamzas, Merlots and Cabernet Sauvignons. The reds in the Rosefield range are quite impressive – full-bodied, with

a distinctly fruity taste, they are clearly aimed at the New World style. Some of the wines marketed under the Maxima brand name are also made here.

Magura Golden Classics: a natural, dry white sparkling wine, deep golden in colour with a slightly greenish tint; intense bouquet with notes of honey and nuts; full-bodied, well-balanced taste; fine, spiralling and long-lasting bubbles.

***Magura* Cabernet Sauvignon 2000**: intense red in colour; rich bouquet with undertones of red forest fruit and oak; well-balanced, firm taste with pleasing warmth and notes of nuts and vanilla.

***Magura* Gamza 2001**: brilliant cherry red in colour; delicate bouquet with the typical varietal hints of raspberries; pleasant fresh taste with a touch of spice on the finish.

***Maxima Rosé FB* Cabernet Sauvignon**: lovely raspberry red in colour; generous bouquet with undertones of cherries and raspberries; full-bodied, pleasantly fresh taste with a touch of spice on the finish.

***Maxima* Chardonnay 2003**: lovely golden colour with a slightly greenish tint; rich nose with tropical fruit and peach enhanced by vanilla; delicate and elegant palate.

Novoselska Gamza Vidin

3700 Vidin, bul. Panonia No. 1, Bulgaria
tel: (+359 94) 601 771, 601 778
e-mail: vin-vidin@mbox.digsys.bg

This winery has cellars in Vidin, and in the villages of Novo Selo and Rouptsi. The vineyards in the area are on the northwestern bank of the Danube, and are mainly under black grape varieties: Gamza, Cabernet Sauvignon, and Merlot. White grapes – Rkatsiteli, Aligoté, and Muscat

Ottonel – are also grown here. The best-known local wine is **Novo Selo Gamza** (also known as **Novoselska Gamza**), of controlled appellation of origin (Controliran). It is made from grapes from controlled vineyards in Novo Selo. It is usually medium-bodied, with distinct acidity and a specific varietal bouquet with hints of forest fruit and a slightly resinous taste. Novo Selo Gamza develops well for up to three or four years, but it is not suitable for long ageing. The winery also offers quality reds from Cabernet Sauvignon, Merlot, and Gamza grapes under its new brand name, **Bononia**.

Vinal – Lovech

5500 Lovech, ul. Al. Koussev No. 37,
Bulgaria
tel: (+359 68) 601 522,
fax 601 527
e-mail: vinal-ad@bitex.bg

Vinal – Lovech specialises in the production of spirits. It also produces white and red table wines from Cabernet Sauvignon, Merlot, Gamza, Dimiat, and Rkatsiteli grapes, marketed mainly under the National Vine and Wine Chamber brand names. The past few years have seen significant investments in vine-growing in the region of Lovech, and this means that the quality of local wines may be expected to improve.

Vinprom Lom

3600 Lom, ul. Belogradchishko Chaussée No. 13,
Bulgaria
tel: (+359 971) 66 666, 66 665, 66 971;
fax: (+359 971) 25 017
e-mail: vinprom@almus.net

This cellar entered the market as an independent producer in the year 2000. It was built in the 1960s, using French models, and supplied with 30-

and 40-tonne ferro-concrete reservoirs. Before it was privatised in 1995, the cellar was owned by the Central Cooperative Union and for quite some time, it was not used for production of wine. In the past few years, it has been thoroughly modernised and remodelled. Its capacity is around 10,000 tonnes. Vinprom Lom produces white and red varietal and blended wines from Merlot, Cabernet Sauvignon, Gamza, Chardonnay, Rkatsiteli, Muscat, Misket, and other grapes. It also offers a range of wines for more discerning clients: Domaine Polomie.

Vinprom Rousse

7000 Rousse, bul. Treti Mart No. 44, Bulgaria
tel: (+369 82) 884 251; fax: (+359 82) 828 289
e-mail: vinery@vinpromrouse.com
www.vinpromrousse.com

This winery was built in its present form in 1967. In 1998 it was sold to the transnational Seaboard Corporation, which invested heavily in technological modernisation in the next two years. From January 2000 to November 2003, Vinprom Rousse was part of the Boyar Estates holding company. It is currently owned by the Russian company Moscow Inter-Republican Wine-Making Plant. Vinprom Rousse has a capacity of around 40,000 tonnes, and subsidiary cellars in Byala and in the village of Dve Mogili.

The conditions in the region are favourable for vine-growing. The cumulative temperature during the growth period is 3,980 degrees Celsius, with a mean temperature of 24 degrees in July. The mean annual rainfall is around 550 mm. Most of the soils are carbonaceous chernozems (humus-rich soil), medium sandy clay, on loess subsoils. The vineyards are in the regions of Rousse and Byala, around the villages of Dve Mogili, Shtraklevo, Tsenovo, and Pirgovo.

The main grape varieties here are Chardonnay, Rkatsiteli, Muscat Ottonel, Dimiat, Sauvignon Blanc, Pamid, and Cabernet Sauvignon. Smaller areas are also under Merlot, Cinsault, and Riesling.

Vinprom Rousse produces a comparatively wide range of whites and reds, the more memorable of which are the Chardonnay, Cabernet Sauvignon, and Merlot limited selections and reserves.

Chardonnay *Limited Selection* 2000: fermented in new Bulgarian oak barrels; lovely golden colour with a greenish tint; impressively rich bouquet with smoky, petrolly and spicy characters; full-bodied, harmonious taste, pleasantly fresh, with undertones of pineapple and melon.

Cabernet Sauvignon *Limited Selection* 2000: deep ruby red; intriguing and rich bouquet suggesting red fruit, spice and minerals; well-balanced body, smooth taste and spicy finish.

Merlot *Limited Selection* 2000: deep garnet in colour; rich bouquet with red fruit, smoke and spice; excellently balanced and intriguing taste that lingers long.

Vinprom Svishtov

5250 Svishtov,
ul. 33-ti Svishtovski Polk No. 110, Bulgaria
tel: (+359 631) 60 470; fax: (+359 631) 60 262
e-mail: vinprom_sv@sv-bg.com

This cellar was established in 1948, and built in its present form between 1954 and 1958. It underwent technological modernisation in the late 1980s. Its capacity is approximately 12,000 tonnes. Vinprom Svishtov has been one of the most popular wineries in recent years. It owns around 450 hectares of vineyards, more than 90% of which are under Cabernet Sauvignon and Merlot.

Vinprom Svishtov produces impressive reds, of which the Cabernets are particularly noteworthy. They are different from the Cabernets in southern Bulgaria – they are lighter-bodied and are closer to those from Burgundy. They are aged in American and French *barriques* for 12–18 months. These Cabernets have blackberries and forest fruit on the nose and they are mellow on the palate, with well-balanced tannins and acidity.

The winery is best known for its **Gorchivka** Cabernet Sauvignon Special Reserve, from controlled vineyards in the Gorchivka area 12 km from Svishtov. It is produced by a classical technique and aged in American and French oak barrels for at least 12 months. This is a classical red, medium-bodied wine, with a well-balanced fruity palate enhanced by mellow tannins and undertones of ripe black fruit, chocolate, vanilla and spice.

***First Flight* Cabernet Sauvignon 2001**: wine from specially selected grapes from the Gorchivka area; aged after fermentation for at least 12 months in American and French oak; deep dark ruby red with a garnet tinge; intense bouquet with notes of overripe red fruit; excellently balanced taste, pleasantly mellow, with a touch of fruit, spice and toast on the finish.

***The Grand River* Rubin & Merlot 2000**: lovely deep red; attractive nose with red fruit, vanilla, spice and smoke; full-bodied and balanced on the palate, with a pleasant aftertaste.

***The Tower of the Wine* Cabernet Sauvignon 1999**: deep ruby red; intense bouquet dominated by ripe red fruit, with slightly spicy notes; full-bodied, well-balanced taste with a pleasantly mellow finish.

Vrachanska Temenouga Wine Cellar

3000 Vratsa, ul. Ledenik No. 57, Bulgaria
tel: (+359 92) 22 464, 61 047;
fax: (+359 92) 61 053
e-mail: vrt@isv.net

This cellar specialises in the production of spirits, but it also makes limited amounts of the white Misket from Vratsa (also known as Vrachanski Misket) specific to the region, as well as white and red table wines.

Institute of Viticulture and Oenology, Pleven

5800 Pleven, ul. Kala-Tepe No. 1, Bulgaria
tel: (+359 64) 22 423, 22 161;
fax: (+359 64) 26 470
e-mail: ilv@lsoft.com

The institute was founded in 1902 as a State Vine and Wine Experimental and Control Station on the initiative of the Ministry of Trade and Agriculture and on the recommendation of Prof. Pierre Viala of France. Its research projects include selection of new varieties, preservation of Bulgaria's vine genetic fund, and development of vine-growing and white and red winemaking techniques. The institute offers varietal vine canes and rootstock and suitable grafting combinations of varieties and rootstock, and designs new vineyards – in other words, it works on all problems related to the quality of vines and wine.

The institute's experimental station comprises two cellars and 60 hectares of experimental vineyards, of which 10 hectares are an ampelographic collection. The old cellar has an extensive wine collection (Oenothèque) of vintages from 1892 to 2002. The new cellar, built in 1971, has a capacity of 1,000 tonnes.

The area lies 134 m above sea level. The climate is temperate continental, with cold winters and hot summers. The mean annual rainfall is 600 mm. The lowest cumulative temperature on record is 3,420 and the highest 4,370 degrees Celsius. The soils are typical and leached to a varying extent carbonaceous chernozems on loess subsoils, medium-heavy to heavy sandy clay, airy, with good water- and heat-retention properties.

The grape varieties grown here are Cabernet Sauvignon, Merlot, Chardonnay, Italian Riesling, Naslada, Misket, Aligoté, Muscat Ottonel, Drouzhba, and Dimiat. The institute produces dry whites and reds for the domestic market only.

Eastern Region (Black Sea Coast)

The Eastern Region stretches along the Black Sea coast, encompassing the Dobrudja plain and the Ludogorie mountains to the northwest and a 25–30 km-wide strip of the southern Black Sea coast. The cumulative temperature during the growth period varies between 3,600 and 4,000 degrees Celsius. Vine growth lasts approximately 210 days, from around 15 April to around 10 November. The mean temperature in July is 21–22 degrees Celsius. The mean annual rainfall is 469–633 mm, and rainfall is 78–89 mm during the grape harvest. The mild climate is favourable mainly for white grape varieties: Dimiat, Chardonnay, Sauvignon Blanc, Ugni Blanc, Muscat Ottonel, Traminer, Rkatsiteli, Riesling, and Aligoté. The conditions in some micro-regions allow cultivation of black grape varieties too: Cabernet Sauvignon, Merlot, and Pamid. The main wineries are in Shumen, Targovishte, Preslav, Khan Krum, Varna, Pomorie, and Burgas.

Black Sea Gold – Pomorie

8200 Pomorie, Promishlena Zona, Bulgaria
tel: (+359 596) 35 332, 32 302, 32 351, 37 003
fax: (+359 596) 32 160
e-mail: office@bsgold.bg
www.bsgold.bg

This is one of Bulgaria's leading wineries. Along with Vincom Burgas, it is currently part of the company Festa Holding. The winery has three cellars in the town of Pomorie and satellite cellars in the villages of Kableshkovo and Bata, and in Nessebar. The oldest cellar (Nessebar) was built in 1932 by the local Dimiat cooperative. The rest were built in the 1950s and 1960s, and modernised over the following decades. Their total capacity is 35,000 tonnes. In the past Pomorie was best known for its light, onion-coloured Pamid.

The local conditions are most favourable for white grape varieties. The mean annual rainfall is around 500 mm, and the cumulative temperature during the growth period approximates 4,000 degrees Celsius. Most of the soils are leached and

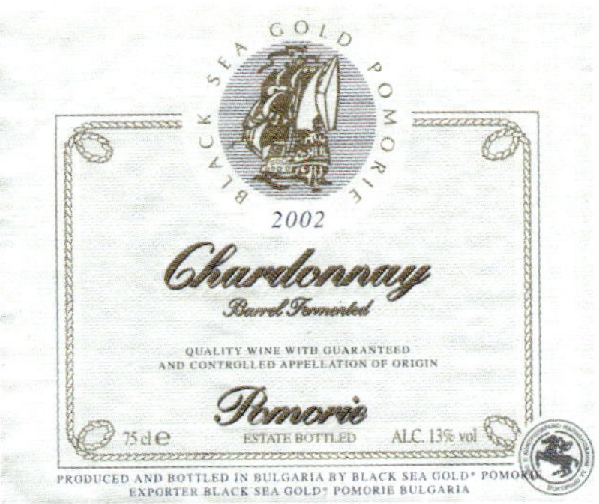

typical chernozem-smolnitz. The vineyards are located in the region of Pomorie, Nessebar, and around Kableshkovo, Bata, Galabets, Goritsa, Poroy, Kosharitsa, Stratsin, and other villages. The most widely cultivated varieties are Chardonnay, Dimiat, Ugni Blanc, Muscat, Rkatsiteli, Sauvignon Blanc, Pamid, Cabernet Sauvignon, and Merlot.

The winery produces mainly white varietal and blended wines, as well as some reds. The local Merlots and Cabernets are usually lighter-bodied. **Barrel-Fermented Chardonnay from Pomorie** is an impressive wine – with a good body, pleasant freshness, citrus and peach on the nose and a mineral note that is peculiar to the region. Some local Muscats and Sauvignon Blancs are also quite popular with wine lovers. The cellar has wine tourism facilities.

***GP Golden Rhyton Chardonnay* 2002**: light golden colour; rich nose with tropical fruit, apples and some vanilla; excellently balanced palate with a pleasantly fresh finish.

Sauvignon Blanc *Pomorie* 2002: lovely straw yellow colour; pleasant, slightly closed nose with herbs and citrus; fresh and elegant palate.

Muscat *Pomorie* 2002: deep golden colour; intense nose with specific varietal undertones of geranium and coriander; full-bodied but mellow and fresh palate.

Dimyat – Varna

9000 Varna, bul. Vladislav Varnenchik No. 281, Bulgaria
tel (+359 52) 5 701 174, 5 701 203, 5 701 144
e-mail: dimyat@triada.bg

Dimyat – Varna is the successor to the Grozd joint-stock company established in 1894, and to several local vine and wine cooperatives that survived until the mid-twentieth century. The old cellar, built in the city centre in the late nineteenth century, is now a tourist attraction. The winery was built in its present form in the 1950s and 1960s. Its capacity is 45,000 tonnes. In 1998 Vinprom Dimyat – Varna was sold to MM Holding. The winery produces mainly white quality and table

wines from Chardonnay, Sauvignon Blanc, Aligoté, Riesling, Ugni Blanc, and Dimiat grapes, as well as some reds from Cabernet Sauvignon and Merlot. It also bottles natural sparkling wines. Part of its products are marketed under National Vine and Wine Chamber brand names. In recent years the winery has also been developing two own brand names, **Bulgari** and **Dimyat Cellar**. The sweet **Snow Wine** from Ugni Blanc grapes has also attracted the attention of a particular category of connoisseurs. The grapes from this wine come from selected south-facing vineyards and are harvested in early winter, when they have shrivelled slightly and have a higher sugar content.

Domaine Boyar Shumen

9700 Shumen, bul. Veliki Preslav No. 71,
Bulgaria
tel: (+359 54) 830 146, 830 149;
fax: (+359 54) 60 525
e-mail: office@shumen.domaineboyar.com

Vinprom Shumen was established in 1948 following the merger of several small local wine cellars. The winery was built in its present form in the 1950s and 1960s, and was subsequently extended. In 1996 it was acquired by Domaine Boyar, which thoroughly remodelled and modernised it over a period of two years.

The climate in the region of Shumen is temperate continental, with hot summers and cold winters. The cumulative temperature during the growth period is around 3,500 degrees Celsius, with a mean temperature of 22 degrees Celsius in July. The best conditions for vine-growing are in the valleys of the Provadiyska and Kamchiya rivers, where there are Black Sea climatic influences. Most of the soils are dark grey forest, highly carboniferous and sandy. In some micro-regions there are also typical carboniferous chernozems. The region is suitable mainly for white grape varieties: Chardonnay, Traminer, Muscat, Sauvignon Blanc, and Dimiat. Cabernet Sauvignon and Merlot are also grown here.

Domaine Boyar Shumen produces a very wide

range of whites and reds, a significant part of which are of controlled appellation of origin: Traminer from Khan Krum, Chardonnay from Shumen, Sauvignon Blanc from Shumen, Muscat from Shumen, and others. Some of Domaine Boyar's prestigious reserves are also made in Shumen.

Chardonnay *Royal Selection* 2003: intense yellow green colour; impressive fruity nose with citrus, apricots and vanilla; well-balanced and mellow palate with a pleasantly fresh finish.

Traminer *Royal Selection* 2003: lovely golden colour with a greenish tint; intense bouquet with hints of flowers, roses, smoke and some citrus; harmonious, full-bodied taste with well-balanced freshness and an elegant, long tropical-fruity finish.

Chardonnay *Barrique* 2003: brilliant deep golden colour; intense bouquet with undertones of citrus, green apples and spice; excellently balanced, fresh and mellow taste that lingers long.

***Muscat from Shumen Region* 2003**: pleasantly straw yellow colour; delicate bouquet with hints of forest flowers; full-bodied, harmonious taste with a lingering finish.

***Traminer from Khan Krum* 2003 (GADO)**: light golden colour with a greenish tint; delicate bouquet with undertones of roses and apples; fresh taste that lingers long.

Khan Krum Winery

9863 s. Khan Krum, obshtina Veliki Preslav, Bulgaria
tel: (+359 5333) 371; fax: (+359 54) 800 200
e-mail: hankrum@mail.bg

The cellar in the village of Khan Krum was built by the local vine-growing cooperative in 1939. Nationalised in 1949, it was part of Vinex Preslav until 2002. Its capacity is around 5,000 tonnes. The

cellar is equipped to process white grapes only, but it can stabilise and bottle both whites and reds.

Until the late 1980s the vineyards in the region exceeded 2,000 hectares but, today, those still suitable for winegrowing are around 700 hectares. This is where Traminer Rosé was introduced in Bulgaria in the 1970s. Most of the soils are moderately leached, sandy clay chernozems, grey forest (in the foothills of the Balkan Mountains), and alluvial-meadow in the Kamchiya river valley. The climate is favourable for cultivation of white grape varieties. The mean cumulative temperature during the growth period is 3,580 degrees Celsius, with a 40–50% probability of being in the range of 3,600–3,900 degrees. The probability of hard frosts (temperatures lower than 20 degrees Celsius below zero) is around 20%. The mean annual rainfall is 586 mm (370 mm during the growth period).

In the recent past the Khan Krum winery was best known for its Traminer of controlled appellation of origin (Controliran). Today it continues to impress also with fine Sauvignon Blancs, Muscats, and Chardonnays, the last of which regularly win prizes at the prestigious Chardonnay du Monde exposition in France.

Khan Krum **Traminer 2002**: light golden in colour, elegant bouquet with the specific varietal notes of roses and flowers, well-balanced taste with a slightly tart finish.

LVK Vinprom – Targovishte

7700 Targovishte,
bul. 29-ti Yanuari No. 8, Bulgaria
tel: (+359 601) 24 751; fax: (+359 601) 24 206
e-mail: manager@lvk-vinprom.com
www.lvk-vinprom.com

This is one of the major wineries on the Bulgarian market. It was established in 1947, with subsidiary cellars in Popovo and Omurtag. Built in its present form in the 1960s, the winery was subsequently extended and modernised. It was named LVK (the Bulgarian acronym for 'Vine and Wine Complex') in 1976. Its current capacity approximates 20,000 tonnes. In the past it was best known for its Eselsmilch, a medium dry white that was especially popular in the former East Germany.

The soils and climatic conditions in the region are more favourable for white wine production. The cumulative temperature during the growth period is approximately 3,700 degrees Celsius, with a mean temperature of around 23 degrees in July. The mean annual rainfall is roughly 600 mm. Most of the soils are humus-carboniferous grey forest. The vineyards occupy an area of around 1,200 hectares, mainly in the region of Targovishte, on hilly terrain in the Balkan Mountains foothills. The most widely planted varieties are Chardonnay, Muscat Ottonel, Rkatsiteli, Traminer, Riesling, Sauvignon Blanc, Aligoté, Cabernet Sauvignon, and Merlot.

The winery produces a wide range of white and red, dry, medium-dry, and sparkling wines, but it is best known among connoisseurs for some of its whites: Chardonnay, Traminer, Sauvignon Blanc, Muscat, and Riesling.

***Targovishte* Sauvignon Blanc**: lovely delicate golden colour with a greenish tint; pleasant bouquet with specific varietal hints of freshly cut grass; delicate body and well-balanced, citrus-fruity taste.

***Targovishte* Chardonnay**: pleasant yellow colour with a soft lemony hue; intense bouquet with notes of pineapple, melon and citrus; well-balanced, pleasantly fresh and lingering taste.

***Targovishte* Traminer**: brilliant straw yellow colour; big nose with ripe fruity and rosy characters; well-balanced, pleasantly fresh palate with a mellow finish.

***Targovishte* Muscat**: pale yellow colour with a slightly greenish tint and sheen; characteristic musky bouquet enhanced by ripe fruit; well-balanced and mellow taste.

***Targovishte* Riesling**: light golden colour with a slightly greenish tint; very rich bouquet with notes of herbs, citrus and peach; well-balanced and elegant taste with a pleasantly fresh finish.

Osmar Wine Cellar

9879 s. Osmar,
obshtina Veliki Preslav,
Bulgaria
tel: (+359 54) 22 074
e-mail: osmar@osmarpelin.com
www.osmarpelin.com

In the 1920s and 1930s, the village of Osmar was synonymous with Bulgaria's best *pelin* (a local white or red wine spiced with herbs and fruit). At the end of the 1990s, the tradition was restored by the brothers

Page 140–141: Osmar Wine Cellar

Dimitri and Vichko Vichev, who built a modern cellar with a capacity of 1,500 tonnes. The cellar produces mainly white and red *pelin*, as well as limited batches of Chardonnay, Merlot, and Cabernet Sauvignon. It has good wine tourism facilities.

Rossenovo Vineyards

8000 Burgas,
ul. Sheynovo No. 32, Bulgaria
tel: (+359 56) 840 805;
fax: (+359 56) 842 875
e-mail: rossenovo@digicom.bg
garancia@hotmail.com

The wine cellar in the village of Rossenovo was built in 1998. It has a capacity of 1,000 tonnes and specialises in the production of red wines fermented in stainless steel vats. It also has a *barrique* ageing section.

The vineyards in the area are around 320 hectares (including 85 hectares of new plantings owned by the winery), mostly around the village of Rossenovo, 35 km southwest of Burgas. The main grape varieties are Cabernet Sauvignon (220 hectares) and Merlot (65 hectares). Small areas are also under Muscat Ottonel and Chardonnay.

The local soils and climatic conditions are favourable for vine-growing, and the region has the potential to produce remarkable wines with their own character and style. Most of the soils are cinnamonic forest, heavy sandy clay, rich in potassium and relatively poor in nitrogen and phosphorus, with a humus content of 2.2–2.5% and a clay content of 30–50%. The region is 200–270 m above sea level. The cumulative temperature during the growth period is approximately 4,000 degrees Celsius, and the mean annual rainfall is around 500 mm.

Sunny Castle Winery

Wine Cellar:
9860 s. Dragoevo,
Shumensko, Bulgaria
Trade Office:
1000 Sofia,
ul. Lavele No. 19, Bulgaria
tel: (+359 2) 987 8902, 981 6951

This cellar was built in 1972 and was a subsidiary of Vinprom Preslav. It was privatised in 2001 and has since been producing wines under its own brand name. It specialises in primary winemaking. The vineyards in the region are around 450 hectares, planted with Chardonnay, Muscat, Traminer, Dimiat, Rkatsiteli, Ugni Blanc, Cabernet Sauvignon, and Merlot.

Sun Valley Winery

Wine Cellar:
7740 s. Nadarevo, Targovishko, Bulgaria
tel: (+359 601) 25 405, 23 726
Trade Office:
1000 Sofia, ul. Lavele No. 19, Bulgaria
tel: (+359 2) 987 8902, 987 1618

This is a new cellar, built in 1998 and specialising in wine stabilisation and bottling. It produces white and red wines from Chardonnay, Muscat, Misket, Sauvignon Blanc, Rkatsiteli, Dimiat, Traminer, Cabernet Sauvignon, and Merlot grapes. It works mainly with the Sunny Castle Winery, but also bottles wine under subcontracts. Since 2000, it has been marketing wines under its own brand name, Sun Valley.

Vincom Burgas

8000 Burgas, p.k. 6, Bulgaria
tel: (+359 56) 880 045, 880 056;
fax: (+359 56) 880 061
e-mail: office@vincom.bg
www.vincom.tetracom-bg.com

This winery was established in 1947. It is currently part of Festa Holding. It has a satellite cellar for primary white winemaking in the town of Aitos. The winery's total capacity is 35,000 tonnes. It has three bottling lines with an aggregate capacity of more than 100,000 bottles a day.

Vincom Burgas produces reds and whites from Chardonnay, Muscat Ottonel, Red Misket, Sauvignon Blanc, Aligoté, Riesling, Ugni Blanc, Rkatsiteli, Dimiat, Pamid, Merlot, and Cabernet Sauvignon grapes. Three local wines were particularly popular in the recent past: **Aitos Muscat**, **Chardonnay de Côte du Sud**, and **Rosé de Côte du Sud**.

***Rosé de Côte du Sud* Cabernet Sauvignon 2001**: lovely cherry red colour; fresh and pleasant bouquet with notes of strawberries and forest fruit; well-balanced and elegant taste.

Young Cabernet Sauvignon: produced by the Beaujolais Nouveau technique; deep dark red in colour; pleasant ripe red-fruity nose; full-bodied and fresh palate typical of young wine.

Vinex Preslav

9850 Veliki Preslav, Promishlena Zona, Bulgaria
tel: (+359 538) 2127, 2588
e-mail: vinex@infotel.bg
www.vinex.bg

In the past this was one of Bulgaria's largest wineries. In addition to quality wine brandy, it is also famous for three excellent whites of controlled appellation of origin (Controliran): **Traminer from Khan Krum**, **Chardonnay from Preslav**, and **Chardonnay from Novi Pazar**. After it was privatised, some of the winery's satellite cellars (in Dragoevo and Khan Krum) developed into independent companies. Today Vinex Preslav continues to produce quality whites and reds mainly from Chardonnay, Traminer, Muscat, Dimiat, Rkatsiteli, Aligoté, Riesling, Cabernet, and other grapes.

***Traminer from Khan Krum* 2002**: lovely brilliant light golden in colour; intense nose with spring flowers and roses; full-bodied and harmonious palate.

***Chardonnay from Preslav* 2002**: brilliant straw yellow in colour; pleasant nose with apple and citrus; harmonious palate with a long and fresh finish.

***Chardonnay & Sauvignon Blanc* 2002**: light yellow colour with a greenish tinge; attractive nose with citrus, peach and freshly cut grass; well-balanced and long palate with a pleasant after-taste.

Vinprom Alvina Dobrich

9300 Dobrich,
bul. 25-ti Septemvri No. 76, Bulgaria
tel: (+359 58) 22 252; fax: (+359 58) 25 698
e-mail:alvina@abv.bg
www.alvina-bg.com

This winery was established in 1947 and built in its present form in the 1960s. In the early 1980s, it became especially popular in Bulgaria for its dry gin produced by the classical technique. Privatised in a management buyout in 1997, it was sold in 2002 to the Varna-based TIM holding company. Vinprom Alvina produces a broad range of white and red dry and medium dry table wines from Misket, Muscat Ottonel, Cabernet Sauvignon, Merlot, and other grapes. Some wines are marketed under the National Vine and Wine Chamber brand names of Sophia, Mecha Krav, and Manastirska Izba. The winery also markets products under its own brand name (Alvina).

Vladimir Distillers Co. – Silistra

7500 Silistra, ul. Tutrakan No. 22, Bulgaria
tel/fax: (+359 86) 22 319, 29 092
e-mail: vladimirdist@yahoo.com
www.vladimirdistillers.com

This cellar was built in 1954 and privatised in the early 1990s. It has a subsidiary cellar in Tutrakan. The winery's total capacity is 17,000 tonnes. The vineyards in the region occupy around 700 hectares, and the conditions are more favourable for white grape varieties.

The winery produces whites and reds from Muscat Ottonel, Riesling, Rkatsiteli, Chardonnay, Feteasca, Cabernet Sauvignon, Merlot, and other grapes. The local wine, Crown of Dobrotitza (Koronata na Dobrotitza; Riesling & Misket), is of guaranteed and controlled apellation of origin.

Wine Cellar Chateau Euxinograde

9000 Varna, mestnost Evxinograd, Bulgaria
tel/fax: (+359 52) 362 098, 363 732
e-mail: euxinogr@techno-link.com

This is Bulgaria's oldest wine cellar. It was built in 1891 and was designed to make quality wine and other alcoholic beverages for the royal palace. Over the following decades, it was repeatedly extended and modernised. In the first half of the twentieth century, the cellar employed some of Bulgaria's best oenologists, who introduced Western wine production techniques and standards in the country. After nationalisation, the cellar was run by the then Security and Protection Department and produced beverages exclusively for the Communist Party and government elite. Today it remains under the administration of the Council of Ministers. The cellar has its own vineyards and produces quality whites from Chardonnay, Aligoté, Traminer, Muscat, Sauvignon Blanc, and other grapes.

Southwestern Region (Struma Valley)

The Southwestern Region covers the area south of Dupnitsa, that is, the Struma river valley. The micro-region around Melnik and Sandanski is most favourable for vine-growing. The comparatively high temperatures (above 4,100 degrees Celsius during the growth period) and the light brown and cinnamonic forest soils of volcanic origin make the region ideal for vine-growing. The vine growth period lasts 220–230 days, from early April to early November. The mean temperature in July is 24–25 degrees Celsius. The most widely planted variety (75% of all vineyards) is Broad Vine of Melnik (Shiroka Melnishka Loza), which grows in this region only. Cabernet Sauvignon, Merlot, and other varieties are also cultivated here. The main wine cellars are in Damianitza, Harsovo, Petrich, Sandanski, and Blagoevgrad.

Damianitza Winery

Wine Cellar:
2813 s. Damianitza, obshtina Sandanski, Bulgaria
tel: (+359 746) 24 114, 22 159;
fax: (+359 746) 24 014
Trade Office:
Sofia, ul. Oborishte No. 22A, Bulgaria
tel: (+359 2) 944 9830, 944 9691
e-mail: damianitza@melnikwine.bg
www.melnikwine.bg

This is one of Bulgaria's most prestigious wineries. It was founded in 1940 by a local vine and wine cooperative. Built in its present form in the 1960s, the winery was privatised in 1997 and subsequently modernised. It has a satellite cellar in the village of Harsovo, and a total capacity of 10,000 tonnes.

The region is ideal for black grape varieties. Most of the soils are weathered cinnamonic forest, sandy soils of volcanic origin. The cumulative temperature during the growth period exceeds 4,100 degrees Celsius, and the mean annual rainfall is around 550 mm. The vineyards are located on hilly terrain mainly around Melnik and the villages of Harsovo, Kromidovo, Marikostinovo, Vinogradi, Lozenitsa, and Hotovo. The indigenous Broad Vine of Melnik prevails (75% of all vineyards), but other varieties – such as Cabernet Sauvignon, Cabernet Franc and Merlot – are also grown here.

In the past the winery was best known for its Melnik Wine from Harsovo. In the last three years it has launched three remarkable reds with a potential for ageing: No Man's Land, Uniqato, and ReDark. Since 2003, it has also been offering quite good wines in its Prestige range.

***ReDark* Merlot**: lovely deep purple colour; blackberries and raspberries on the nose; long body with a harmonious structure and excellently balanced soft tannins.

***No Man's Land* Cabernet Sauvignon & Merlot**: lovely ruby red colour with a violet tinge; complex bouquet with undertones of red forest fruit, blackberries, vanilla and toasted bread; excellently balanced mellow and long taste with fruit on the finish.

***Uniqato* Early Vine of Melnik**: deep red colour; rich bouquet with hints of morello cherries, blackberries and spice; harmonious and impressive taste with notes of vanilla, smoke and herbs; pleasant spicy finish; an excellent wine.

Melnik Wine from Harsovo: deep garnet red; rich bouquet with the typical varietal hints of cherries, tobacco, leather and spice; excellently balanced taste that is pleasantly tart and with a wisp of vanilla on the finish.

Mira Wine Cellar, Sandanski

2800 Sandanski, ul. Svoboda No. 49, Bulgaria
tel: (+359 0746) 32 255, 24 585

This cellar was built in 1993 and has a capacity of around 2,000 tonnes. It gets its grapes from the region of Petrich and Sandanski. It produces bulk and bottled reds and whites from Cabernet Sauvignon, Merlot, Broad Vine of Melnik, Muscat Ottonel, Sauvignon Blanc, and Keratzuda grapes. The winery is known on the home market for its Melnik Reserve, Cabernet Reserve, Melnik 55, and Keratzuda from the Kresna region.

St Nicola Melnik Winery

Wine Cellar:
2850 Petrich, Promishlena Zona, Bulgaria
Trade Office:
1000 Sofia, ul. Dunav No. 13, Bulgaria
tel: (+359 2) 980 3648, 980 1628
e-mail: stnicola@datacom.bg

This is a new cellar. The St Nicola brand name was launched on the market in 1999. The winery produces whites and reds from Broad Vine of Melnik, Cabernet Sauvignon, Merlot, Chardonnay, and other grapes. It is aiming to move more upmarket with some wines from its Ecstasy range.

Sub-Balkan Region (Rose Valley)

The Sub-Balkan Region extends from the southern slopes of the Balkan Mountains to the northern slopes of the Sredna Gora Mountains, encompassing Karlovo, Sungurlare, Slavyantsi (sometimes spelled 'Slaviantzi'), Karnobat, Sliven, and the neighbouring villages. The mountains obstruct climatic influences from the north and south, and create specific local conditions for vine-growing. The cumulative temperature during the growth period is almost 4,000 degrees Celsius, with a mean temperature of 22.2 degrees in July. The mean annual rainfall is around 650 mm, rarely exceeding 90 mm in September and October. The most widely planted variety here is Red Misket, which yields the popular whites of controlled apellation of origin Sungurlare Misket and Rose Valley Misket. Among the other varieties grown here are Cabernet Sauvignon, Merlot, and Chardonnay.

Chateau Ruko

8800 Yambol, Bulgaria
tel: (+359 4714) 570, 525
e-mail: chateau_ruko@yahoo.com

This is a brand-new cellar, built in 2001 under a EU-financed project. It has its own vineyards (200 hectares) and produces white and red table wines from Merlot, Cabernet, Chardonnay, and Muscat grapes. In 2003 the winery launched two own brand names, Spartacos and Kabile.

***Kabile* Chardonnay Barrique 2002**: straw yellow colour; pleasant bouquet of citrus with a wisp of oak; harmonious and pleasantly fresh taste.

***Kabile* Merlot Barrique 2002**: deep ruby red; very rich bouquet with hints of ripe red and black fruit complemented by vanilla and spice; well-balanced and mellow taste.

Domaine Boyar Blueridge – Sliven

8800 Sliven, Industrialna Zona, Bulgaria
tel: (+359 44) 662 570, 662 590, 642 471
e-mail: db@sl.bia-bg.com
www.domaineboyar.com

This winery is the most modern one in Bulgaria and among the most modern ones in Europe. It was built in 1999 by the joint-stock company Domaine Boyar (the leading exporter of Bulgarian wine to Western Europe in the last ten years) and designed by A&G Engineering of Australia. Its annual output of reds and whites exceeds ten million litres. The state-of-the-art equipment allows application of a very wide range of techniques and total control over production. With its separate production lines, Domaine Boyar Blueridge practically has the potential of several smaller wineries and can produce small batches of wines with an individual character and style. It has more than 2,000 Bulgarian, French, and American oak *barriques*.

The winery gets its grapes mainly from the southeastern vine-growing region, where most of

the soils are medium-heavy to heavy sandy clay cinnamonic forest, alluvial-meadow, and smolnitz soils, with a humus content of 2–4%. In the separate micro-regions the mean cumulative temperature during the growth period varies between 3,900 and 4,060 degrees Celsius, and the mean annual rainfall between 580 and 600 mm. The main grape varieties cultivated here are Cabernet Sauvignon, Merlot, Chardonnay, Dimiat, and Muscat.

The winery produces a wide range of red and white quality and table wines. On the home market, it is best known for its Blueridge Cabernet, Merlot, and Chardonnay.

Chardonnay Grande Selection 2003: intense golden colour; attractive nose with melon, toasted bread and honey; mellow, full-bodied and harmonious palate with some spice and vanilla on the finish. This wine won a Gold Rhyton at the 2004 Vinaria International Exhibition of Vine-Growing and Wine-Producing, Bulgaria.

Merlot Grande Reserve 2001: deep ruby red showing some development on the rim; intriguing bouquet with hints of plums, cherries, green peppers and violets, complemented by a resinous undertone; well-balanced and firm taste with notes of red fruit, tobacco, herbs and black pepper.

Cabernet Sauvignon Grande Reserve 1999: deep ruby red colour with a slightly brickish tint; generous nose with black fruit, oak and leather characters; well-balanced and firm palate with a touch of spice on the finish.

***Blueridge* Cabernet Sauvignon**: attractive deep red colour; pleasantly fruity with raspberries and blackcurrants on the nose; excellently balanced on the palate.

***Blueridge American Barrel* Merlot**: deep ruby red; fruity and spicy nose; full, long body with a good structure and a touch of chocolate and vanilla on the finish.

***Blueridge* Chardonnay**: lovely light golden colour; rich nose with peach, apples and honey; full-bodied, harmonious palate with a pleasantly fresh finish.

***Oravinifera* Cabernet Sauvignon 1999**: well-preserved ruby red colour with some development on the rim; intense and warm nose with ripe red fruit, smoke and spice; full-bodied, harmonious palate with a long and pleasantly spicy finish.

Korten Wine Cellar

s. Korten, obshtina Nova Zagora, Bulgaria
tel: (+359 4522) 20 22;
fax: (+359 4522) 20 23

This cellar is part of the Domaine Boyar company. It has a capacity of around 5,000 tonnes and facilities for white and red wine production. The cellar has three wine-ageing rooms with 2,300 American and French oak *barriques*, in addition to its own barrel-making workshop. Since 2003, Korten has been producing exclusively single-vineyard boutique wines. The grapes are picked by hand in crates and fermented in oak fermenters (600 litres) along with a submerged manta. The varieties used are Merlot, Cabernet Sauvignon, and Mavrud.

Old Cellar 1924 – Yambol

8600 Yambol, ul. Matvey Vulev No. 75,
Bulgaria
tel: (+359 46) 62 532
e-mail: oldcellar@.jambol.bse.bg

This cellar was built in 1924 by the local Misket Vine and Wine Cooperative. Curiously, most of the cooperative's founders were people with urban and, moreover, intellectual professions: teachers, doctors, a photographer, bank clerks, and traders. The cellar, built under a Belgian design, is constructed entirely of stone. In 1949 it was nationalised, functioning as a subsidiary of Vinprom Yambol (sometimes spelled 'Iambol' or 'Jambol') in the next four decades. In 1993 the cellar was privatised and has since been restored to its original form. Its capacity is 2,000 tonnes. It has oak barrels (seven or eight tonnes each) for wine storage as well as *barriques*. The cellar produces quality reds mostly from Cabernet Sauvignon and Merlot, as well as limited amounts from Mavrud and Pinot Noir.

Rose Valley Winery – Karlovo

Wine Cellar:
4300 Karlovo, ul. Beshbunar No. 1, Bulgaria
tel: (+359 335) 94 450
Trade Office:
1000 Sofia, ul. Racho Dimchev No. 1, Bulgaria
tel: (+359 2) 988 2018, 988 5936
e-mail: c.v.r.@mail.orbitel.bg
www.rosevalleywinery.com

This cellar was established in 1927 by the Karlovski Misket Vine and Wine Cooperative and the Bank for Agricultural Credit. In the past the region was best known for the local white Misket from Karlovo. Today the winery produces varietal and blended reds and whites mainly from Chardonnay, Karlovo Misket, Muscat, Cabernet Sauvignon, and Merlot grapes. Two of its wines are of note: Cabinet and Rhapsody. Since 2001, the winery has been managing the royal residence

in the village of Banya, using the royal family crest and developing its own brand name – Royal Collection.

***Cabinet* Cabernet & Merlot**: deep, dark ruby red and vibrant colour; warm, with red forest fruit, plums and dried leaves on the nose; mellow and harmonious on the palate.

***Rhapsody* Merlot & Cabernet**: lovely colour with a garnet tinge; attractive bouquet with hints of blackcurrant, oak and plums; full-bodied, harmonious and excellently balanced taste with notes of vanilla and red fruit in the aftertaste.

SYS Industries LTD

Wine Cellar:
8473 s. Venets, Karnobatsko,
Bulgaria
tel: (+359 559) 26 11, 60 18
Trade Office:
1407 Sofia, bul. James Boutcher No. 87,
Bulgaria
tel: (+359 2) 962 2030
e-mail: sysind3@netel.bg

This company is known mainly as a producer of spirits, but since 1998 it has also been investing in wine production. Its current grape-processing capacity is around 10,000 tonnes. It gets most of its grapes from the region of Karnobat, and produces reds and whites from Cabernet Sauvignon, Merlot, Pinot Noir, Chardonnay, and Muscat. In 2003, SYS Industries launched two own brand names: Chateau Karnobat and Romanza.

***Chateau Karnobat* Chardonnay 2002**: brilliant deep yellow colour with a slightly greenish tinge; citrus on the nose; well-balanced and fresh on the palate.

***Romanza* Merlot Reserve 1999**: deep ruby red; interesting bouquet with notes of red fruit, spice and oak; full-bodied, firm taste with distinct freshness, a long and slightly spicy finish.

***Romanza* Cabernet Sauvignon Reserve 1999**: intense ruby red colour; pleasant bouquet with ripe red fruit, vanilla and spice; well-balanced taste with a pleasantly dry finish.

Vinarska Izba – LVK Grozden

Wine Cellar:
s. Grozden, obl. Burgaska, Bulgaria
tel: (+359 5571) 21 59
Trade Office:
1303 Sofia, bul. Hristo Botev No. 80, Bulgaria
tel: (+359 2) 931 0487, 931 1114
e-mail: grozden@internet-bg.net
www.rakia.com

This is an old cooperative cellar which became an independent producer after it was privatised. It entered the market with several kinds of high-quality grape *rakiya* in 1998. In the last two years, it

has been aiming to impress connoisseurs with two challenging Cabernets: Aristocrat and Autumn Magic.

***Aristocrat* Cabernet Sauvignon Reserve 2001**: deep garnet colour; attractive bouquet with hints of forest fruit and vanilla; firm taste with a slightly tart finish.

Vinex Slavyantsi

8460 s. Slavyantsi, obshtina Sungurlare,
obl. Burgaska, Bulgaria
tel: (+359 5571) 25 00, 23 48
fax: (+359 5571) 22 17
e-mail: office@vinex.bg.com
www.vinexbg.com

This is one of Bulgaria's prestigious wineries. It was established in 1950 on the basis of several older vine and wine cooperatives in Slavyantsi, Padarevo and Sungurlare. The conditions in the Sungurlare valley are very favourable for vine-growing – it is less than 250 m above sea level, and has a mean annual rainfall of around 570 mm and light sandy clay, cinnamonic forest soils. The cumulative temperature during the growth period is approximately 3,700 degrees Celsius. The region has a comparatively mild winter, warm summer, and long, dry autumn. The vineyards are compact and located mainly on the southern slopes of the hills. Red Misket, Chardonnay, Muscat Ottonel, Italian and German Riesling, Sauvignon Blanc, Dimiat, Traminer,

and Ugni Blanc are grown here. The most widely cultivated black grape varieties are Cabernet Sauvignon, Merlot, Pinot Noir, and Syrah.

The winery has a total of five cellars in Sungurlare, Slavyantsi, Lozarevo, Chernitsa, and Karnobat. Its annual capacity is around 15,000 tonnes of wine and *rakiya*.

Vinex Slavyantsi produces a wide range of wines, the whites being the more memorable variety. It makes some of the best Bulgarian Chardonnays – with a generous floral bouquet and apple freshness enhanced by hints of honey and bananas when barrel-fermented or oak-aged. **Sungurlare Misket** is of guaranteed and controlled apellation of origin. It has a fine varietal bouquet elegantly enhanced by undertones of apricots, wild strawberries and honey. More noteworthy among the reds is the young Pinot Noir, as well as the Cabernet and Merlot from the **Chateau Slavyantsi** range.

***Rose Creek* Pinot Noir**: light ruby red; impressive nose with ripe cherries and blackcurrants; very pleasant mellow palate with preserved fruit; an excellent wine.

***Chateau Slavyantsi Rosé* Cabernet Sauvignon**: deep strawberry colour; attractive nose with forest fruit and cherries, well-balanced palate with a pleasantly fresh finish.

Vini Sliven

8800 Sliven, ul. Tsar Simeon No. 59, Bulgaria
tel: (+359 44) 667 666, 667 117; fax: (+359 44) 662 388
e-mail: office@vini.bg-bg.com
www.vini.bg

This has become one of Bulgaria's leading wineries in recent years. Vini Sliven is the successor to the local Shevka Wine Cooperative, founded in 1920, as well as to other local wine cooperatives. It was built in its present form in the 1960s, and subsequently extended and modernised. It has satellite cellars in Nova Zagora, Shivatchevo, Blatets, and Padarevo. Their total capacity is 80,000 tonnes.

Most of the soils in the region are diluvial- and alluvial-meadow and leached cinnamonic forest. The cumulative temperature during the growth period approximates 3,800 degrees Celsius, and the mean annual rainfall 600 mm. Black grape varieties prevail (60% of all vineyards): Cabernet Sauvignon, Merlot, Pamid, and Pinot Noir. The main white grape varieties are Misket, Muscat Ottonel, Chardonnay, Rkatsiteli, Aligoté, Dimiat, and Traminer.

The local reds (Cabernet and Merlot) are most memorable – they are southern in style, full-bodied, mellow and well-balanced on the palate, with forest fruit, blackcurrants and blackberries on the nose. Some wines are aged in French and American oak.

Valley of the Roses is a very good rosé, with strawberries and raspberries on the nose and fruit on the palate. Some special selections of Chardonnay are of note too – with citrus, peach and honey on the nose and a well-balanced, pleasantly fresh palate. The wines from the **Balkan Crest** and **Tuida** ranges are also doing quite well on the market.

Balkan Crest **Cabernet Sauvignon Reserve 1999**: deep garnet colour; interesting bouquet dominated by red fruit, dried leaves, oak and spice; mellow and pleasant taste with nuts and dried fruit on the finish.

Tuida **Cabernet Sauvignon**: deep ruby colour; pleasant bouquet dominated by red stone fruit and spice; well-balanced taste.

Chateau Shivatchevo **Cabernet Sauvignon 2001**: deep garnet colour; attractive bouquet with undertones of smoke, vanilla and forest fruit; harmonious taste with hints of nuts and vanilla on the finish.

Southern Region (Thracian Plain)

The Southern Region spans a large area around Plovdiv, Pazardjik, Haskovo, Harmanli, Liubimec, and Stara Zagora. The cumulative temperature during the growth period varies between 3,700 and 4,000 degrees Celsius. Vine growth starts in the first week of April and ends in the first week of November. The mean temperature in July is 23 or 24 degrees. Winter frosts are comparatively rare. The mean annual rainfall is 530–650 mm; rainfall is 80–90 mm during the grape harvest. The soils and climate are suitable mainly for black grape varieties, such as Cabernet Sauvignon and Merlot. The unique Bulgarian variety Mavrud is grown in limited areas around Assenovgrad, Pazardjik and Peroushtitsa. Merlots from Haskovo, Stambolovo, Liubimec and Ivailovgrad are especially popular, along with Cabernets from Stara Zagora. Other varieties grown here include Pamid, Muscat Ottonel, Dimiat, and Rkatsiteli. The principal wineries are in Peroushtitsa, Brestovitza, Assenovgrad, Haskovo, Liubimec, and Stara Zagora.

Brestovitza Winery Nov Jivot

4224 s. Brestovitza, obl. Plovdivska, Bulgaria
tel: (+359 3142) 22 21, 22 23

This French-designed cellar constructed entirely of stone was built in the 1930s by the local vine and wine cooperative. It later became a subsidiary of Vinprom Pulden – Peroushtitsa. After it was privatised, it was thoroughly modernised, and it has developed as an independent company. The winery specialises in red wine. It makes some of

the best Bulgarian wines from Cabernet Sauvignon, Merlot, Rubin, and Mavrud grapes. The **Erigone** and **Maximinus Thrax** ranges are especially popular with Bulgarian connoisseurs.

***Erigone* Cabernet Sauvignon 1999**: deep ruby red colour; well-developed bouquet with undertones of red fruit, smoke, spice and vanilla; well-balanced taste with a pleasant and long finish.

Cabernet Sauvignon *Brestovitza* 2000: deep ruby red colour; generous bouquet with distinct red fruit; well-balanced taste with a firm structure.

Brezovo Winery

4160 Brezovo, ul. Vassil Kolarov No. 18,
Bulgaria
tel (+359 3191) 2726, 2271, 2311
e-mail: ricom_bg@hotmail.com

This winery in the vicinity of the town of Brezovo was built in 1958. The hilly terrain along the southern slopes of the Sredna Gora mountains, combined with chernozem and cinnamonic forest soils, is very favourable for vine-growing and winemaking. The climatic conditions are also favourable, because the local air currents do not allow retention of cold air masses in winter. In the past the area was best known for its local wine from Brezovo Misket. Until 2000, this winery was a subsidiary of Vinprom Pulden – Peroushtitsa. It has a capacity of 1,200 tonnes and produces white and red varietal wines from Cabernet Sauvignon, Merlot, Mavrud, Red Misket, Chardonnay, and Muscat grapes.

Domain Menada, Stara Zagora

6002 Stara Zagora, ul. Hadji D. Assenov No. 1,
Bulgaria
tel: (+359 42) 38 459; fax: (+359 42) 629 269
e-mail: domain.menada@belvedere.bg
www.belvedere.bg

This winery was established in 1947 by combining two vine and wine cooperatives dating back to the 1920s, Loza and Sila (from the village of Oriachovitza). In the 1970s and 1980s, Vinprom Stara Zagora was modernised, incorporating the cellars in the villages of Oriachovitza and Dalboki, and in the towns of Kazanlak and Liubimec. The region grows mostly black grape varieties, especially Cabernet Sauvignon and Merlot. In recent decades, it has become known as the producer of some of the best Bulgarian wines of controlled appellations of origin (Controliran) – such as Oriachovitza Cabernet Sauvignon, Oriachovitza Merlot, and Old Red from Oriachovitza – which have won prizes at prestigious international exhibitions.

In 1990 the winery was renamed Menada PLC – Stara Zagora, and it was privatised four years later. It was acquired by its present owner, the Belvedere Group of France, in October 2002. In 2003 and 2004, the cellar was thoroughly remodelled with a grant of EUR 4.5 million from EU funds. It is currently one of Bulgaria's most modern cellars.

Most of the soils in the region are cinnamonic forest, medium and light sandy clay. The climate is temperate continental, with an early spring and a late autumn. The cumulative temperature during the growth period is around 4,000 degrees Celsius, and the mean annual rainfall is approximately 600 mm. The mean temperature in July is 24 degrees. The region is located at an altitude of 170–260 m above sea level. The vineyards occu-

py around 1,200 hectares – mostly in the villages of Oriachovitza, Bratya Kunchevi, Dalboki, Kolena, Hrishteni, Bogomilovo, Kirilovo, and Trakiya – facing south at an inclination of 3–6 degrees. The most widely cultivated varieties are Merlot, Cabernet Sauvignon, Pamid, Rkatsiteli, Aligoté, and Dimiat.

Domain Menada produces a wide range of quality and table wines, mainly reds. Its Cabernet Sauvignon Reserve is quite impressive.

***Tcherga* 2002**: a blend of Merlot, Rubin and Cabernet Sauvignon; garnet colour with a soft brickish tinge; intense bouquet of wild forest fruit with a touch of vanilla and spice; a big taste with a good structure and a mellow finish; an impressive wine.

***Traiana* Cabernet Sauvignon 2001**: lovely cherry red colour with some development on the rim; intense and very attractive nose with hints of spice, autumn leaves, oak and resin; mellow and harmonious palate with distinct spicy freshness and an elegant finish.

***Augusta* Merlot 2001**: deep ruby red; rich and complex bouquet dominated by ripe red fruit and spice; excellently balanced and smooth taste with soft tannins and a warm, red-fruity finish.

Old Red from Oriachovitza: ruby red colour with a brickish tinge; attractive bouquet with notes of raspberries, dried fruit, autumn leaves and vanilla; well-balanced taste with soft tannins and a long and pleasant aftertaste.

***Oriachovitza* Cabernet Sauvignon Reserve**: produced by the cellar in the village of Oriachovitza from grapes from the southern slopes of the Sredna Gora mountains, and aged in Californian oak; rich and impressive bouquet with distinct spice and a touch of resin; mellow and elegant taste that lingers long.

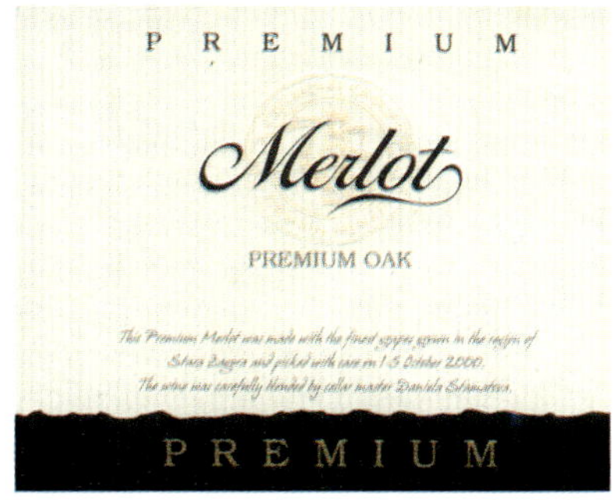

***Domain Menada* Merlot**: ruby red colour; intense plummy and dried-fruity bouquet; harmonious, mellow taste with a good body.

Domain Sakar

6550 Liubimec, ul. Shar Planina No. 2,
obl. Haskovska, Bulgaria
tel: (+359 3751) 42 27; fax: (+359 3571) 21 44
e-mail: sakar@lubimetz.com

This is one of Bulgaria's most successful wineries in recent years. Until 1991, it was owned by Vinprom Haskovo. Its present owner is the French company Belvedere. The winery has a capacity of around 15,000 tonnes. The region of Liubimec (sometimes spelled 'Lubimetz' or 'Lyubimets') offers very favourable conditions for growing Merlot and Cabernet Sauvignon, from which in the past three years Domaine Sakar has produced some wines that have been rated highly at prestigious exhibitions in Bulgaria and abroad.

Domaine Sakar wines have a good body and distinctly fruity character. Their bouquet is dominated by ripe grapes, enhanced by a light vanilla undertone. The taste is well-balanced and mellow, with a pleasant spicy finish.

***Domain Sakar* Merlot Reserve 2000**: deep garnet red colour with development on the rim; attractive nose with dried fruit, spice, vanilla and cara-

mel; excellently balanced palate with a firm structure and a long aftertaste dominated by dried fruit.

Domain Sakar **Cabernet Special Reserve 1999**: deep, intense colour; big nose with juicy red fruit and spice; harmonious and smooth palate with a fresh finish.

Domain Sakar **Cabernet Premium 2002**: lovely soft ruby colour; generous nose with black fruit and blackcurrant; pleasantly mellow palate.

Domain Sakar **Merlot Special Selection 1997**: deep red colour with some development on the rim; attractive nose with red fruit, spice and vanilla; elegant palate with a slightly spicy finish.

Estate Santa Sarah

tel: (+359 457) 27 101; fax: (+359 457) 22 655
www.santa-sarah.com

Santa Sarah is a cellar on wheels. The small team of enthusiastic winemakers has for the last few years been based in rented premises at the old wine factory in Nova Zagora, and runs its operations in three caravans. This unconventional winemaking concept is the brainchild of Ivo Genovski, a Bulgarian wine trader. In the late 1990s, he tried to introduce to Bulgaria a practice which had long been dictating wine fashions in the West – limited

Ivena Commerce Winery Dolna Banya

Head Office:
2040 Dolna Banya,
ul. Targovska No. 1,
Bulgaria
tel: (+359 7120) 23 40
Trade Office:
1407 Sofia,
bul. James Boutcher No. 116,
Bulgaria
tel: (+359 2) 963 0753, 963 0793

This winery launched its brand name in the late 1990s. It has subsidiary cellars in the villages of Karabunar, near Pazardjik, and Boboshevo, near Kyustendil. Ivena produces white and red table wines for a very wide range of consumers. Since 2002, it has been developing a new brand name, Chateau Ivena.

release top-class wines produced without compromising on quality. Santa Sarah works only with small private vine-growers from southern Bulgaria. It uses Cabernet Sauvignon, Merlot, and Rubin grapes. The yield is limited to 4,000 litres per hectare. The grapes are picked by hand in crates. The wines are fermented in small (10–50 hectolitres) oak and stainless steel fermenters and aged in oak at a constant temperature of 12 degrees Celsius for 8–18 months. They are then bottle-aged for another 12 months before finally being released on the market. Santa Sarah has a total annual capacity of 25,000 wooden crates (12 bottles each). It has 500 new *barriques* from French, Californian, Bulgarian, German, and Austrian oak. In the next few years, Genovski's team plans to establish a true wine estate with its own elite vineyard in the vicinity of the village of Goritsa, near Nessebar.

Pamidovo Thracian Winery

Wine Cellar:
4459 s. Pamidovo, Pazardjishko,
Bulgaria
tel: (+359 3526) 29 72
Trade Office:
Sofia, bul. Tsarigradsko Chaussée No. 2,
Bulgaria
tel: (+359 2) 870 3414;
fax: (+359 2) 873 4375
e-mail: office@pamidovo.com
www.pamidovo.com

This new, state-of-the-art winery was built in 1999. Some of the wines are aged in Bulgarian *barriques*. The winery has a capacity of around 2,000 tonnes and gets its grapes from the villages of Pamidovo, Karabunar, and Velichkovo. The soils here are mostly cinnamonic forest, light, and rich in potassium and phosphorus. The terrain is hilly and the climate is good for vine-growing, with constant air currents that prevent retention of cold air masses in winter. The cumulative temperature

during the growth period approximates 3,900 degrees Celsius, and the mean annual rainfall is 550 mm. The winery produces varietal and blended wines from Cabernet Sauvignon, Merlot, Mavrud, and Pamid grapes. It also offers Chardonnay, Muscat, and Dimiat under its own brand name. In May 2001, some of its reds were rated highly at the Pro Wein exposition in Düsseldorf.

Thracia Estate Wine Company

Wine Cellar:
s. Granit, obshtina Bratya Daskalovi
Trade Office:
1000 Sofia, ul. Frityof Nansen No. 17
tel: (+359 888) 842 086
e-mail: trakia_estate@yahoo.com

The village of Granit lies in the centre of the Upper Thracian Plain, 40 km to the east of Plovdiv and 20 km to the south of Chirpan. The conditions in this region are favourable for vine-growing and winemaking. Most of the local vineyards are on the southern slopes of the Sredna Gora mountains. This wine cellar was built in 1971 and was used mainly as a storehouse of the state-owned wine corporation Vinprom. The cellar was privatised in 2001. It has a capacity of around 2,400 tonnes and produces mainly red wines from Cabernet Sauvignon, Merlot, and Mavrud grapes.

Todoroff Wine Cellar

Wine Cellar:
4224 s. Brestovitza, ul. Gen. Gurko No. 1, obl. Plovdivska, Bulgaria
tel: (+359 3142) 24 88
Trade Office:
1421 Sofia, bul. Vassil Levski No. 83, Bulgaria
tel: (+359 2) 985 4785, 985 4786
e-mail: office@todoroff-wines.com
www.todoroff-wines.com

In the past three years, this cellar has been one of the most frequently cited examples of the new trends in the Bulgarian wine industry. It was built in 1945 by the Andonov Brothers and nationalised less than two years later. In 2001, building entrepreneur Ivan Todoroff bought the cellar from the heirs of the original owners and converted it into a state-of-the-art boutique winery. It has a capacity of 200 tonnes and produces only small batches of quality reds from Cabernet Sauvignon, Merlot, and Mavrud grapes.

The region around the village of Brestovitza (sometimes spelled 'Brestovica') is ideal for red wine production. The cumulative temperature during the growth period exceeds 4,000 degrees Celsius, and the mean annual rainfall is around 550 mm. Most of the soils are brown cinnamonic, with a loose, sandy clay structure. They contain around 40% clay, 20% gravel, 3% humus and more than

Todoroff Wine Cellar

100 mg/kg iron compounds. The vineyards are on southwest-facing hilly terrain at an inclination of 12–15 degrees Celsius. The grapes are selected and picked by hand, invariably in crates.

The cellar offers varietal wines from Cabernet, Merlot and Mavrud grapes in three ranges: **Boutique**, **Teres**, and **Gallery**. Todoroff Boutique wines are impressive for their full-bodied but mellow and excellently balanced taste with a good length. Teres wines are a special selection. They are aged in Bulgarian and American oak *barriques* for 6–10 months, and then bottle-aged. Their bouquet is rich and fruity, with the specific undertones of the respective variety, enhanced by spicy and toasty flavours developed through the contact with oak. Todoroff Gallery wines are barrel-aged for 5 months. In 2004, Todoroff also produced limited batches of Cabernet Sauvignon Rosé and Chardonnay. The winery has excellent wine tourism facilities.

Villa Vinifera Wine Cellar

4224 s. Brestovitza, obl. Plovdivska, Bulgaria
tel: (+359 3142) 23 53, (+359 32) 624 011
e-mail: starho@plov.omega.bg
www.wine-cellar.dir.bg

Built in 1936, this cellar was owned by the local wine merchant Metodi Hadjiyankov. Nationalised in the late 1940s, it was sold in 1998 to the Plovdiv-based company Starho. The cellar has a capacity of around 400 tonnes. It uses exclusively oak containers and applies classical (traditional) winemaking techniques. Villa Vinifera produces limited batches of whites (Misket, Dimiat, Muscat, and Rikat) and reds (Cabernet, Merlot, and Mavrud), of which the latter are more noteworthy.

Vinivel Ltd – Ivailovgrad

Head Office:
6570 Ivailovgrad,
ul. Kapitan Petko Voivoda No. 18, Bulgaria
tel: (+359 32) 652 028; fax: (+359 32) 652 026
Trade Office:
Plovdiv, ul. Raiko Daskalov No. 72, Bulgaria
e-mail: vinivel@dir.bg

This winery was built in 1971 by the state-owned wine corporation Vinprom. Since the year 2000, it has belonged to Yulian and Ivana Yamantiev. Thoroughly remodelled and modernised under a EU-financed project in 2002, the winery complies with all quality-control requirements. It has a capacity of around 2,000 tonnes, and produces mainly Cabernet Sauvignon and Merlot, as well as some Chardonnay. Vinivel wines are full-bodied and harmonious, with a distinctly fruity taste and character. The soils and climatic conditions in the region of Ivailovgrad are very favourable for black grape varieties. Most of the soils are leached cinnamonic forest, rich in limestone. The cumulative temperature during the growth period exceeds 4,000 degrees Celsius. The micro-region is exposed to Aegean climatic influences. A constant air current prevents retention of hot air in summer and cold air in winter. The vineyards occupy an area of around 250 hectares, mostly under black grape varieties.

Vinivel exports bulk wine to the UK and bottled wine to the USA. In 2003 it launched three own brand names: Villa Armira, Paralel 41, and Yamantiev's.

Vinprom Haskovo

6300 Haskovo, Industrialna Zona, Bulgaria
tel: (+359 38) 661 611, 31 771
e-mail: chataida@haskovo.ttm.bg

In the late 1970s and 1980s, Vinprom Haskovo was one of Bulgaria's most prosperous wineries. It largely owed its fame to the Merlot grape variety, which grows very well in the Maritsa river valley, where Haskovo is located. The winery was best known for two wines of controlled appellation of origin (Controliran) that are still quite popular: **Merlot from Sakar** and **Stambolovo Merlot**. In autumn 2003, Vinprom Haskovo and its

satellite cellar in the village of Stambolovo were acquired by the holding company Novico Wine & Spirits Group, which also owns the cellars in Chirpan, Parvenets, and Levski.

The best vineyards in the region are on hilly terrain, mostly facing south, around the villages of Stambolovo, Tsareva Polyana, Kralevo, Momkovo, Mustrak, and Dimitrovche. The most widely planted variety is Merlot (70%), but Cabernet Sauvignon (10%) and other grapes are also grown here.

The soils are light sandy clay. The cumulative temperature during the growth period approximates 4,200 degrees Celsius, and the mean annual rainfall is 600 mm.

Vinprom Haskovo produces quality and table reds mostly from Merlot and Cabernet Sauvignon grapes, and some whites from Rkatsiteli, Dimiat, and Muscat.

Vinprom Peshtera

Head Office:
4550 Peshtera, ul. Georgi Kyosseivanov No. 1, Bulgaria
tel: (+359 350) 23 43, 37 87
Trade Office:
4000 Plovdiv, ul. Shesti Septemvri No. 113, Bulgaria
tel: (+359 32) 641 685
e-mail: vinprom@mobicom.com

Vinprom Peshtera is the successor to the local cooperative cellar established in 1939. In the past, this region was known for its well-developed viticulture. In the last few years, however, Peshtera has come to be associated mainly with the production of spirits. Brighton Distillers Group Ltd of the UK holds a 48% stake in the company. Significant investments in its modernisation were made in 2002 and 2003. At present, Vinprom Peshtera has a capacity of around 14,000 tonnes, owns 120 hectares under vines and plans to plant new vineyards. In summer 2003, it bought Vinprom Yambol. In addition to spirits, the company offers dry whites and reds from Cabernet Sauvignon, Merlot, and Sauvignon Blanc grapes in two ranges, Bacchus and Peshtera.

Vintechprom Pazardjik

4400 Pazardjik,
ul. Milyo Voyvoda No. 6,
Bulgaria
tel: (+359 34) 446 373;
fax: (+359 34) 446 350
e-mail: vintech@pasat.bg

This winery is the successor to an old local vine and wine cooperative. It was built in its present form in the 1960s. It produces whites and reds from Cabernet Sauvignon, Merlot, Mavrud, Pamid, Red Misket, Rkatsiteli, and Aligoté grapes under its own brand names as well as under National Vine and Wine Chamber brands. Its most impressive wine in recent years is **Pazardjik's Old** (Controliran), a blend of Merlot, Mavrud and Pamid.

Vinzavod Assenovgrad

4230 Assenovgrad, bul. Bulgaria No. 75,
Bulgaria
tel: (+359 331) 22 240

The region of Assenovgrad (sometimes spelled 'Asenovgrad') has always been best known for the indigenous variety Mavrud. This winery was established in 1947 following the merger of several small private cellars. It was built in its present form in the 1950s and 1960s. Its capacity is 12,000 tonnes.

Most of the vineyards in the region are located on the low slopes of the Rhodopi mountains around Assenovgrad, Parvenets, Proslav, Markovo, Belashtitsa, Brestnik, Kuklen, Cherven, Topolovo, and Novakovo. Most of the soils are cinnamonic forest, chernozem-smolnitz, and alluvial-meadow. The cumulative temperature during the growth period exceeds 4,000 degrees Celsius, and the mean annual rainfall is around 550 mm (350 mm during the growth period).

The winery produces red wines only – mainly Mavrud (of controlled appellation of origin), Cabernet Sauvignon, and some Merlot.

Mavrud *Gold Rhyton* 2001: deep ruby red colour; distinct varietal bouquet with hints of red forest fruit; full-bodied, mellow taste with a good structure and a long finish.

Mavrud Reserve 1998: ruby red colour with a brickish tinge; distinct varietal bouquet enhanced by oak; full-bodied, mellow taste with an attractive finish.

Cabernet *Plovdiv* 2001: dark red colour; distinct varietal bouquet; full-bodied, smooth and warm taste.

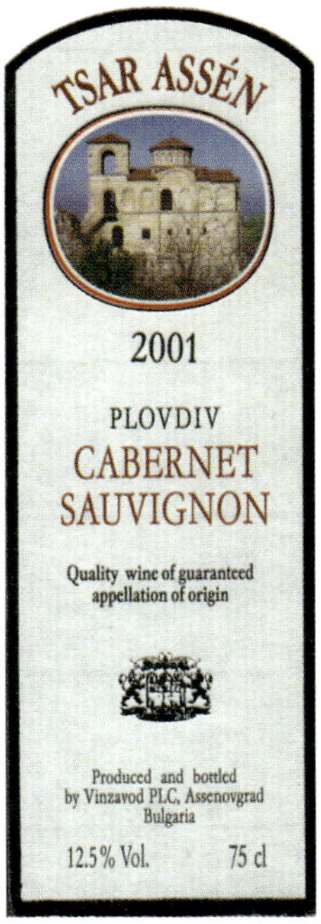

***Assenovgrad Mavrud* 1997 (Controliran)**: deep ruby red; closed nose with spice and vanilla; well-balanced palate with a pleasantly mellow finish.

***Maxima* Mavrud Reserve 1998**: attractive deep red colour; very rich nose with ripe red fruit and spice discreetly complemented by vanilla; excellently balanced, full-bodied palate with preserved fruit and a pleasantly spicy long finish; an impressive wine.

***Maxima* Mavrud 2000**: brilliant deep garnet; generous bouquet dominated by ripe red and black fruit with a touch of vanilla; well-balanced, firm fruity taste with a long and pleasantly spicy finish.

Wine Cellar Pulden Peroushtitsa

4225 Peroushtitsa, obl. Plovdivska, Bulgaria
tel: (+359 32) 624 446, (+359 3143) 26 30, 23 70
e-mail: pulden@mail.bg
wine_cellar_peroushtitsa@mail.orbitel.bg
www.pulden.f2s.com

The original cellar was built in the 1930s by the local vine and wine cooperative. According to an agricultural business survey from the period, at that time there were 600 hectares of vineyards

around Peroushtitsa (sometimes spelled 'Perustica'), and the local vine-growers had 399 sprayers – which was quite impressive by local standards. New workshops were built in the 1960s and 1970s. Pulden's total capacity, including two satellite cellars for primary winemaking in the village of Brestnik and the town of Saedinenie, exceeds 30,000 tonnes. Since 1962, the cellar has also been producing natural sparkling wines. In the year 2000, it was sold to Industrial Holding Bulgaria.

The cellar produces mainly reds from Cabernet Sauvignon, Mavrud, Merlot, and Rubin grapes, as well as some whites from Muscat, Chardonnay, and Rkatsiteli.

One of its best-known products is **Wine from Brestnik** (of controlled appellation of origin) – a blend of Cabernet, Merlot and Mavrud with a mellow and spicy taste and a rich, forest-fruity bouquet. Some of its wines from Mavrud, Cabernet Sauvignon, and Rubin grapes are quite good too. Pulden also offers collection wines.

Rubin *Pulden Peroushtitsa* 2000: lovely ruby red colour; closed nose with black forest fruit; full-bodied, well-balanced palate with a firm structure and a spicy finish.

Wine House Vinogradez

4487 s. Vingradez, Pazardjishko, Bulgaria
tel: (+359 3568) 22 21

This is an old cooperative cellar which produced bulk whites and reds from Cabernet Sauvignon, Merlot, Pamid, Rkatsiteli, Dimiat, and Muscat Ottonel grapes. In 2003, it was bought by the businessman Petar Mandjukov and soon after started marketing bottled wines under two new brand names: Ars Magica and Romance. The winery plans to move its products (Cabernet, Merlot, and Mavrud) more upmarket. The region around the village of Vinogradez (sometimes spelled 'Vinogradec' or 'Vinogradets') is very favourable for vine-growing, so that winery undoubtedly has a future.

National Vine and Wine Institutions

National Vine and Wine Chamber
1000 Sofia, ul. Lavele No. 19, Bulgaria
tel: (+359 2) 981 0574, 981 0849, 981 1674
tel/fax: (+359 2) 988 4797
e-mail: awine@mb.bia-bg.com
www.bulgarianwines.org

The National Vine and Wine Chamber (NVWC) is an inter-professional organisation of the producers, processors and traders in grapes, wine, and grape and wine products. Its mission is to protect the professional interests of its members; to protect and control the origin, quality and authenticity of the goods produced and traded; and to develop viticulture and winemaking.

The NVWC has five regional chambers based in Plovdiv, Pleven, Sliven, Varna, and Blagoevgrad. The Regional Vine and Wine Chambers (RVWCs) maintain a register of producers of wine grapes and quality wine, issue certificates of origin for quality wines and certificates of authenticity for grape *rakiya* and wine brandy, and appoint regional tasting boards to perform compulsory organoleptic analysis and evaluation of wines, grape *rakiya* and wine brandy.

The NVWC approves and implements a strategy for the development of viticulture, winemaking, and trade in wine, and vine and wine products.

The NVWC and RWVCs are non-governmental organisations whose purpose is to contribute to the development and competitiveness of Bulgaria's vine and wine sector.

An important element of the NVWC's activi-

ties is the Vinaria International Exhibition of Vine-Growing and Wine-Producing, co-organised by the Plovdiv International Fair. Vinaria, launched in 1992, is the largest specialised exhibition in south-eastern Europe. This annual exhibition is preceded by NVWC-organised national wine-, *rakiya*– and wine brandy-tasting sessions. The Vinaria prizes are the most prestigious awards within the professional community.

The NVWC boasts an impressive collection (Oenothèque) of 35,000 bottles of wines awarded at Vinaria. The collection gives a good idea of the development of Bulgarian winemaking in recent years.

The NVWC publishes a bimonthly magazine, *Vine-Growing and Winemaking*, the only specialist vine and wine periodical in Bulgaria. The magazine serves not only as a forum for Bulgarian vine-growers and winemakers but also as a window on international trends in the industry. In addition to academic articles, it offers extensive information on trade, legal, economic and technological issues.

The NVWC holds the intellectual property rights to several popular Bulgarian brand names: Sophia, Mecha Krav, Vecherny Zvon, Zolotaya Osen, Stary Gorod, and Zolotoy Bereg. These brand names may be used only by wine producers who are members of the NVWC and have signed licensing contracts.

National Wine and Spirituous Beverages Research Institute
1618 Sofia, bul. Tsar Boris III No. 134, Bulgaria
tel: (+359 2) 955 5360; fax: (+359 2) 955 5361
e-mail: office@wineinbg.org
www.wineinbg.org

This institute was established in 1952. It has state-of-the-art laboratories and offers solutions to a wide range of practical problems that could arise in the course of wine production. Its key priorities are monitoring, analysis and evaluation of wines; it also compiles a database on production management. The institute develops regulations on wines of guaranteed apellation of origin and wines of guaranteed and controlled apellation of origin. It also offers design services ranging from individual facilities to entire production units.

Vine and Wine Executive Agency
1113 Sofia, bul. Tsarigradsko Chaussée
No. 125, bl. 1, et. 3, Bulgaria
tel: (+359 2) 970 8111, 970 8101, 970 8106

Indexes

BULGARIAN CELLARS

BULGARIAN WINES

International Exhibition of Vine-Growing
and Wine-Producing
Wine Festival
National Wine and Spirits Tasting

VINARIA, the International Exhibition of Vine-Growing and Wine-Producing and Wine Festival, is the largest in scale and most important specialized event staged within the sector in Central and Southeastern Europe. VINARIA is a world-renown exhibition event. It has been included in the calendar of UFI – The Global Association of the Exhibition Industry since 1997.

VINARIA

Business and fairyland.

Labour and wisdom.

Tradition deeply rooted in ancient times.

Vinaria is a festivity.

Vinaria smooths the way for you.

Wine is a festivity.

The wine festivity is called

VINARIA.

The most impressive, prestigious

and splendid!

Bulgarian viticulturists and vintners

created VINARIA and it is the hallmark

of their industrious labour and

the emanation of their mastery.

EXHIBITION SCOPE OF VINARIA

- Wines and other alcoholic beverages
- Vine-growing and wine-producing
- Equipment and machinery for vine-growing and grape harvesting
- Preparations for plant protection and fertilizers
- Equipment for grape processing, stabilization and bottling of wines and other alcoholic beverages
- Information, consulting, marketing, research and development in the field of vine-growing and wine-producing

Vinaria

"WINE AND LOVE,

LOVE AND WINE" Ball

A spectacular Ball of Enologists is staged during VINARIA.

Here, graduates of institutes of higher education in the field of viticulture and wine production take a Dionysian oath and are inaugurated to the branch.

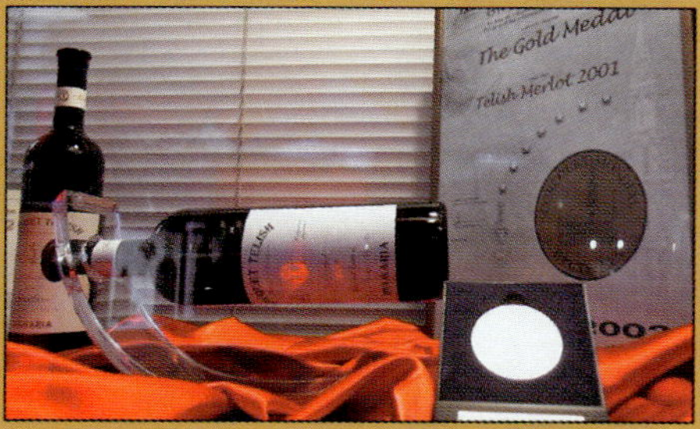

National Tasting Sessions, within the Wine Festival, feature the most reputable contest staged to assess Bulgarian wines and alcoholic beverages.

The best wines in four categories receive the unique "Golden Rhyton" prize awarded by International Fair – Plovdiv. The jury awards gold, silver and bronze medals, honorary diplomas and "Wine of the Year" diplomas – valuable dividends for a wine producer.

THE BEST BULGARIAN "GOLDEN RHYTON" AWARDED WINES

	WINE VARIETY	VINTAGE	PRODUCER
VINARIA 1996	Puldin Cabernet x Mavrud	1989	Vinprom Plovdiv Ltd., Peroushtiza
	Cabernet Sauvignon Bitter, Special Reserve	1993	Vinprom Svishtov Ltd., Svishtov
	Merlot from Sakar	1991	Vinprom Haskovo Ltd., Haskovo
	Traminer	1994	LVK Vinprom Ltd., Targovishte
	Sauvignon Blanc	1995	Vinex Preslav Ltd., Veliki Preslav
	Cabernet Sauvignon	1995	Vinprom Haskovo Ltd., Haskovo
VINARIA 1997	Dunav Prista Chardonnay	1996	Vinprom Rousse JSC, Rousse
	Merlot – 10	1996	LVK Gamza, Suhindol
	Chardonnay	1995	Vinprom Rousse JSC, Rouse
	Mavrud	1987	Vinzavod JSC, Assenovgrad
VINARIA 1998	Novi Pazar Chardonnay – Barrique AOC	1997	Vinex Preslav JSC, Veliki Preslav
	Rousse Chardonnay	1995	Vinprom Rousse JSC, Rousse
	Cabernet – 26	1997	LVK Gamza, Suhindol
	Stambolovo Merlot, Barrique	1996	Vinprom Haskovo Ltd., Haskovo
VINARIA 1999	Trimontium Sauvignon Blanc	1998	LVK Vinprom JSC, Tagovishte
	Mavrud – 24 Declared Geographic Region	1998	LVK Gamza, Suhindol
	Chardonnay – 8 Declared Geographic Region	1997	LVK Gamza, Suhindol
	Cabernet R	1992	Vintechprom JSC, Pazardjik
VINARIA 2000	Merlot 1	1999	SNS JSC, Stamboliiski
	Chardonnay 5 – Declared Geographic Region	1999	LVK Gamza, Suhindol
	Merlot 34 Declared Geographic Region	1996	LVK Gamza, Suhindol
	Chardonnay Barrique 2	1998	Vinex Slavyantsi JSC, Slavyantsi
VINARIA 2001	Chardonnay I	2000	Black Sea Gold JSC, Pomorie
	Cabernet Sauvignon IV sample	2000	Vini JSC, Sliven
	Chardonnay Barrique	1998	Vinex Slavyantsi JSC
	Merlot	1997	Sakar Winery JSC, Lyubimets
VINARIA 2002	Chardonnay Batch IV	2001	Black Sea Gold JSC, Pomorie
	Assenovgrad Mavrud Type 3	2001	Vinzavod JSC, Assenovgrad
	Targovishte Traminer	2000	LVK Vinprom JSC, Targovishte
	Oryahovitza Cabernet Sauvignon, Special Reserve	1998	Menada JSC, Stara Zagora
VINARIA 2003	Chardonnay, Pomorie Region – Batch X	2002	Black Sea Gold JSC, Pomorie
	Southern Coast Rose	2001	Vincom JSC, Bourgas
	Tuida Cabernet Sauvignon	2002	Vini JSC, Sliven
	Cabernet Sauvignon, Special Reserve, Bitter	1998	Vinprom Svishtov JSC
VINARIA 2004	Chardonnay, Regional Table Wine, Sliven Region, Batch 1	2003	Domaine Boyar JSC, Sliven Branch
	Cabernet Sauvignon, VIII	2003	Vincom JSC, Bourgas
	Targovishte Chardonnay	2001	LVK Vinprom JSC, Targovishte
	Slavyantsi Chardonnay	1998	Vinex Slavyantsi JSC
	Domaine Boyar Merlot Thracian Lowlands	2001	Domaine Boyar JSC, Sliven Branch

Yassen Borislavov

Bulgarian
WINE BOOK

Translated by **Katerina Popova**
English Editor: **Rumen Mitkov**
Copy Editor: **Joe Garver**
Designer: **Lyudmil Vesselinov**
Art Editor: **Viktor Paunov**
Photographs: **Maria Ninova, Nadezhda Chipeva, Georgi Nikolov**
Production: **Stanislav Ivanov**

office@trud.bg
www.trud.cc

First edition
Format 8/60x90. Printer's sheets 23.5

TRUD PUBLISHING HOUSE

Printed in Bulgaria by Dimitar Blagoev Printing Co., Ltd.

TRUD BOOKSHOPS:
136 Vassil Levski Blvd., Sofia, Bulgaria
63 Skobelev Blvd., Sofia, Bulgaria